OTHER BOOKS BY JAY R. LEACH

How Should We Then Live
Behold the Man
The Blood Runs Through It
Drawn Away
Give Me Jesus
A Lamp unto My Feet
Grace that Saves
The Narrow Way
Radical Restoration in the Church

Radical

Restoration
in the
Church

Restoring the True Faith for the Final Hour

J A Y   R .   L E A C H

Order this book online at www.trafford.com
or email orders@trafford.com

Most Trafford titles are also available at major online book retailers.

Scripture is taken from the New King James Version, Copyright 1979, 1980,
1982, 1997 and 2007 by Thomas Nelson, inc. unless otherwise noted.

Scripture quotations identified KJV are from the Scofield Reference Bible,
Copyright 1909, 1917, 1937, 1945, 1996 by Oxford University Press, Inc.

Printed in the United States of America.

ISBN: 978-1-4907-5349-2 (sc)
ISBN: 978-1-4907-5350-8 (e)

Trafford rev. 01/21/2015

www.trafford.com
North America & international
toll-free: 1 888 232 4444 (USA & Canada)
fax: 812 355 4082

CONTENTS

SECTION IV
BODY LEADERSHIP

SECTION V
DISCIPLEING THE NEXT GENERATION

SECTION SIX
RESTORE!

This book is dedicated to our Lord and Savior, Jesus Christ and all sincere believers who desire to be watchmen who equip others with a viable biblical worldview through the power of the Gospel of Jesus Christ. May God bless you as you study and internalize these truths and teach them to others, who in turn will teach yet others in Jesus' name!

INTRODUCTION

"**M**ake disciples!" "Teach them" to observe all things that I have commanded you ……." that is the mandate of our Lord and Savior, for all believers (see Matthew 28:19-20). "As you sent Me into the world,' I also have sent them into the world. I in them, and You in Me; that they may be made perfect in one, and that the world may know that You have sent Me, and have loved them as You have loved Me" (John 17:18, 23).

For two thousand years this commission has been the biblically clear known will of God – and a priority one mission for the church; yet, many churches are busy "making" religious converts, enlisting members to fill the pews and other motives coupled with unnecessary secular add-ons. Therefore, their true kingdom purpose of discipling others, [winning people to Christ and bringing them to full maturity in the body of Christ], has been totally forfeited or put on the back burner which equates to the next generation being raised up without Christ.

Additionally this has resulted in many people in the emerging generations coming into their charge promoting the idea that the great commission has outlived its usefulness; and is no longer the priority for the church. In the first place that thinking robs others of the spiritual benefits of a biblical worldview and Christian consensus. Thus, local governmental agencies, academia, and the media experience very little resistance promoting their secular humanistic worldview [of no God] and their atheistic consensus [man is the measure of all things]. This deceptive concept has left many churches filled with natural talent, entertainment, a flurry of programmed religious activities and fleshly forms of godliness that deny the power of God. In his book, *Understanding the Times,* author David Nochel said it this way, "A biblical worldview is based on the infallible Word of God. When you believe the Bible is entirely true, then you allow it to be the foundation of everything you say and do."

This is quite essential as young church leaders seem to overlook the spiritual accomplishments and holy examples of prior generations as they exhibit an inordinate attachment to the culture of their own generation rather than reflecting the intergenerational love and wisdom of the church in all times and everywhere.

The question is asked, "How does a biblical worldview get denied, as has happened in America? The answer is found in the promotion of the secular worldview that bombards us constantly from public education, television, films, music, newspapers, magazines, books, academia and many pastors, teachers and other church leaders who do not have, nor promote and teach viable biblical worldview. It has been said,

---

"The church does have a Man in heaven, Jesus Christ, but many have lost sight of Him."

Unless a radical move is made to restore a biblical worldview, unity and New Testament concepts in the churches – many of our churches will ignorantly forgot their God-given purpose for existence. The truth of this statement has already manifested itself in marriages, families and other biblical institutions across the nation. We may ignore it, but that only makes it worse. *"Where there is no vision the people perish"* (Proverbs 29:18).

Our risen Lord left this primary mission for the church until He returns. Prior to leaving He demonstrated the concept, model, and spiritual requirements for those who make up His Church. Jesus' life, death and resurrection cast a new model for human lives, a new *spiritual creation, "one new man,"* the New Testament Church, the body of Christ [Jew and Gentile together], making spiritually mature disciples – who exist to carry out the continuing mission of Jesus. He demonstrated that you have done nothing for the kingdom of God until you have been instrumental in *changing* the lives of others. How? Paul says that believers are *"living letters from Christ."* Written "By My Spirit said the Lord" (see Zechariah 4:6), on tablets of human hearts. Living letters that can be read by all men (see 2 Corinthians 3:2-3).

The Disciple's Secret Weapon

Jesus described the Holy Spirit as the One *"whom the world cannot receive, because it neither sees Him nor knows Him; but you know Him, for He dwells with you and will be in you"* (John 14:17). *"But you shall receive power when the Holy Spirit has come upon; and you shall be witnesses to Me in Jerusalem, and in all Judea and Samaria, and to the end of the earth"* (Acts 1:8). This meant that the Holy Spirit was and continues to be the Christian's "secret weapon" for launching an invincible worldwide witnessing and evangelism campaign for the Kingdom of God.

Every Spirit-filled believer is to be launched through the Holy Spirit's influence into all of life's commitments and relationships. Often my wife and I are approached by people asking: "Where do you get the strength and power to do these things?" "How can I gain that experience?" It involves:

- Loving the Lord and others
- Truly hearing and obeying the Word
- Learning and developing a viable biblical worldview
- Seeing the Word lived out in others
- Choosing to obey and do the Lord's will
- Enjoying a personal experience of God's presence and power

Such an awakening comes only when the Holy Spirit radiates from Spirit-filled lives. The Scripture substantiated this truth in the lives of the twelve disciples after Pentecost. Once the power of the Holy Spirit was released in their lives the disciples moved from weak, wobbly, and wavering to aggressive and irresistible Christ followers. The disciples were ordered to wait until this *supernatural* power of the Holy Spirit came upon them before attempting their *supernatural* mission in the world.

Once they *experienced* the Holy Spirit their impact on society was so great that they were referred to as the instruments that *"turned the world upside down"* (Acts 17:6).The Apostle Peter stands out as a vivid example of a person both before and after experiencing the fulfillment of the promised Pentecost! He later exclaimed to them, "Repent, and let every one of you be baptized in the name of Jesus Christ for the remission of sins; and you shall receive the gift of the Holy Spirit. For the *promise* is to you and to your children, and to *all who are afar off,* as many as the Lord our God will call" (Acts 2:28-29). Emphasis is added throughout:

- Repentance and baptism are our responsibilities.
- The gift of the Holy Spirit is the Lord's responsibility.

Notice the Word of God said, "You *shall receive* the gift of the Holy Spirit." Webster's New Explorer Dictionary defines the word "shall" as an auxiliary to express a command.[1] God said it so that settles it! The Holy Spirit puts us in communion with the Father and the Son; therefore, we are placed *in* Christ.

The indwelling Spirit is also fulfillment of the *New Covenant* whereby God's law is written on our hearts (see Jeremiah 31:33, 34). Not only are our sins forgiven, but the Lord has placed His law within us. All of this accomplished through the finished work of Jesus Christ, our Lord, *"For by grace you have been saved through faith and that not of yourselves; it is the gift of God, not of works, lest any man should boast"* (see Ephesians 2:8).

In Romans 5:5, the Apostle Paul speaking of Christ's model of the new born again believers,

> *"The love of God*
> *has been poured out in our hearts*
> *by the Holy Spirit*
> *who*
> *has been given to us."*

We will explore this truth more fully throughout the book. One major hindrance to the Spirit's working within the church occurs when the church is thought of as an institution rather than what it truly is, an organism. The institutional approach to the Christian life *gradually robs us* of the awareness of the *supernatural.* A radical supernaturalism is imperative in our approach to life as part of every Christian's existence for a viable church and life of godliness.

Much of the religious fervor and frustrating activities of many local churches have totally circumvented the Spirit's ministry amongst their membership. The void created by this denial of the Spirit and biblical worldview has been filled with individual and blended worldviews, "feel good" entertainment, show choirs, a class of super-star ministers, worldly influenced dancing and other activities in the name of praise and worship. None of it is spiritually related to the teaching of "those things that the Lord commanded ..."

For this very reason more and more believers are becoming disheartened with their local churches today. Nothing happens there that can't be accomplished without the supernatural power of God! Such forms by denying the power of God fosters an atmosphere that leaves the people drained, hungry and thirsty for true reality seeking a restoration of God's revealed truth.

Most of those leaving simply desire authentic involvement in God-honoring, Bible-believing churches. If the church in America is to survive for future generations – it must radically restore its kingdom focus of making true spiritually maturing Christ followers! The first church service was conducted on the Day of Pentecost in Jerusalem with Peter under the anointing of the Holy Spirit preaching the sermon.

The tremendous response to that Spirit-powered sermon was three thousand souls, who heard and received the Word. The Holy Spirit led the disciples to set the precedence for what this new-born church of 3,120 Spirit-filled believers did to implement the disciple-making process immediately. Notice, Acts 2:42 says,

> *"They were continually*
> *devoting themselves*
> *to*
> *the apostles' teaching*
> *and to fellowship,*
> *to the breaking of bread*
> *and to prayer."*

So the first church began with four essentials which provide a description of what the church did. *Radical restoration* must be marked by a sharp *departure* from the non-essential business as usual attitudes, traditions and customs. How? Through Spirit-led changes in existing secular views, practices, habits, concepts and models. The Holy Spirit is strongly speaking to the churches to initiate a paradigm shift from being church-centered to kingdom centered! Church leadership is admonished to "hear what the Spirit is saying to the churches" (see Revelation 2:29).

We must obediently return to doing these basic four essentials; in spite of other demands that may be added. If one of these essentials is left off, then that church is not the kind of church Jesus promised to build. The disciples, the body of Christ, remain responsible based on the mandate left us by our Lord to ["make disciples" and "teaching them to do all..."], that they may reproduce themselves in others. For too long the church has made this "teaching" a matter of head knowledge which produces converts or members, but not heart knowledge which produces mature soul-winning disciples.

To make converts or members instead of fully equipped disciples as commanded by our Lord is fatal to the health and life of your church!

– Jay R. Leach

To restore the original intent of the "teaching" we must include a practical experience component to make the disciple ready through spiritual exercise, proficiency, and skill [with the effects of the gospel working in their lives]. Therefore,

- New disciples must be *trained* in the biblical worldview [the faith].
- New disciples must be *trained* in the fellowship of the church.
- New disciples must be *trained* in the breaking of bread (Communion).
- New disciples must be *trained* in the discipline of prayer.
- New disciples must be *trained* in intergenerational communications.
- New disciples must be *trained* witnesses for Christ.
- New disciples must be *trained* through small-group ministry.

Participation in corporate prayers was viewed as an essential part of the spiritual growth of the new *disciple* as part of the whole church. Jesus said, "A disciple is not above his teacher, but everyone who is perfectly *trained* will be like his [or her] teacher" (Luke 6:40). This first church was large, yet manageable. There were no customs and traditions; there were no constitution and by-laws, no secular-enhanced programs nor division because the Holy Spirit was welcome and in control!

Amazing things happen in the church when ordinary men and women are led and anointed by the Spirit of God. Like the Apostle Paul's message; our message cannot be with wise and persuasive words, *but with a demonstration of the Spirit's power,* so that your faith might not rest on men's wisdom, but on God's power. We are good at teaching straight sound doctrine from the Scriptures, but for hearts and lives to be changed – we need the power of God!

Radical Restoration in the Church will expand your vision for what God can and will do, and inspire you to pray and witness like never before for the power of the Spirit in your church – and in you! The church for the most part has been compromised through a secular worldview; which is so prevalent in American culture today.

"Righteousness exalts a nation, but sin is a reproach to any people" (Proverbs14:34).

As a result, throughout this book you will see that what we once commonly called a biblical worldview and Christian consensus is eroding and very subtly being replaced with a set of twins born in academia, a secular humanistic worldview and hedonistic/ materialistic consensus. In most places today, the conduct and experience of professing Christians are very different from early power-packed Christ followers.

Today they meet regularly in the church building for worship; they live decent, respectable lives; they conduct themselves displaying the utmost integrity; they arouse no opposition. *But they make little if any impact* in the community and marketplace in which they live and work. Therefore, *ignorance* and *indifference* toward spiritual things will prevail, unchecked, unchanged and unchallenged!

The majority of their neighbors and fellow workers neither know nor care what these Christians believe or why they attend church. That's why we find ourselves in a world that is anti-church and certainly disconnected from biblical knowledge of the truth.

In spite of the on-going, crippling spiritual erosion that we are experiencing in the Christian community; Christ has promised that He will build His church and the gates of hell will not prevail against it! We are encouraged with the rich history of the early church; which provides a pattern for us to restore the truth and fervor of Pentecost.

Church history proves that the church is at its best – when the world is at its Worst!

Christ will be triumphant in the end, and those witnessing disciples who stand with Him and live for Him will be victorious. That's good news!

It is my sincere prayer that those who read this book will be free indeed to be faithful disciples, who help save and teach others who in turn will save and teach still others. We must join Christ in the greatest challenge the church worldwide has ever faced. As Spirit-filled disciples we are to watch and pray. Then as Christ's agents of restoration, we are to help others during these perilous times – to insure that His people will have faith for the final hour!

– Jay R. Leach
Fayetteville, North Carolina

SECTION I

HE IS LORD OF ALL

BUT SEEK FIRST THE KINGDOM OF GOD
AND HIS RIGHTEOUSNESS,
AND ALL THESE THINGS
WILL BE ADDED TO YOU. (Matthew 6:33)

HE IS LORD OF ALL

HE IS LORD

He is Lord, He is Lord, He is risen from the dead and He is Lord;
Every knee shall bow, every tongue confess,
That Jesus Christ is Lord.
– Unknown

HAVE THINE OWN WAY, LORD!

Have thine own way, Lord! Have thine own way!
Thou art the Potter, I am the clay:
Mold me and make me, after thy will,
While I am waiting, yielded and still.

-- George C. Stebbins

I enlisted in the U.S. Army at the age of eighteen and retired after serving twenty six and one half years. One thing drilled into me upon entering the Army that remained prevalent throughout my career [*individually and corporately*] was the fact that I was now a G.I. which meant Government Issue. I was no longer my own – I belonged to the U.S. Government, the "green machine" we were "ONE" [period]. Fully committed; I was willing to give my life. I could put nothing before my government including my wife and children. No matter what we planned, it was subject to be changed by the will of the Army.

As we left Army life in 1984, I was called to the first of three Baptist churches in southeastern North Carolina which the Lord allowed me to pastor over the past 28 years. By His grace, in 1998 while still in full-time pastoral ministry; my wife and I were led by the Spirit to plant the Bread of life ministries and plant the Bread of Life Bible Institute which today is one school in eight locations. Our mission is equipping the saints through the disciple-making process of ["one new man"] in Christ!

Additionally the Lord has used us as His instruments in helping to plant five disciple-making churches. Twenty seven ministries are out growths of the teaching and experiencing of the truth of God's Word at the Bread of Life. As Christ's disciples – we have fully committed our lives to our Lord and the expansion of His kingdom. In the military, receiving orders from above, I had to go anywhere in the world the government sent me, on some occasions leaving my loved ones behind. I could put nothing before my commitment to Uncle Sam. It was an exciting and very enjoyable experience for my family and me.

We loved Army life, especially the travel and especially experiencing the Christian churches among the people in the different cultures wherever assigned throughout the world. Knowing that I could deploy on short notice – we lived at the ready. When I did deploy even to Vietnam, life in the Leach family kept rolling along. Homecoming always meant family vacation which on one occasion was two weeks on Waikiki beach in Hawaii [that was certainly a rarity in those days]. Every new assignment was a great family adventure.

My wife stood with me for twenty one and a half of my years in the military raising and making Christ followers of our five children. Our military career came to an end thirty years ago. Sometimes it's such a joy as we sit back and reminisce over our fifty-two years together. Our life commitment to the Lord is much more critical and much more enjoyable in Christ, than Uncle Sam. We committed ourselves to Uncle Sam; surly we are even more fully committed to the Lord's work. For the past sixteen years, the Bread of Life has been on the offense for the kingdom of God!

"Not by might nor by power, but by My Spirit said the Lord." Oh! What a blessing!

"And the things that you have heard from me among many witnesses, commit these to faithful men who will be able to teach others also" (2 Timothy 2:2).

The Great Commission

I stated in the introduction, "Make disciple" and "teach them" is the two-fold commission from our Lord (see Matthew 28:19-20). Jesus gave the commission to His twelve disciples *[trained by Him]*. He expected His disciples to see the world as He saw it – through them and the disciples they would produce. Christ's vision for us to reach the world is through the multiplying of disciples. This plan of multiplication found in 2 Timothy 2. Paul admonishes Timothy and each true born again Christian,

> *"And the things you have heard from me*
> *among many witnesses,*
> *commit these to faithful men*
> *who will be able*
> *to teach others also."*

Paul told young Timothy that he saw something in him and decided to invest in him. It indicates the deposit of a sacred trust. In other words, you are my disciple. This is the relationship between you and me. We are to commit to the same.

Commit to faithful men [and women]

Now you commit it to others. To do this means we transmit not only what we know, but more importantly what we are. It is important to note, each of us becomes like the people we associate with. Later Paul wrote to him, "But you have carefully followed my doctrine, manner of life, purpose, faith, longsuffering, love, perseverance, persecutions, afflictions, which happened to me …" (2 Timothy 3:10, 11). "Yes and all who live godly in Christ Jesus will suffer persecution" (v. 12).

Therefore, what Paul commits to Timothy is to be given to faithful men [and women]. Faithful men and women are not always easy to find. God still seeks them. Are you one of His faithful? "But evil men and imposters will grow worse and worse, deceiving and being deceived. But you must continue in the things which you have learned and been assured of knowing from whom you have learned them" (2 Timothy 3:13-14).

Teach others also

Here is where the rubber meets the road; and the disciple-making process is able to move forward in faith. Notice we are now in the *fourth generation*. Paul is the first generation, then came Timothy, then "faithful men" and now "teaches others also":

- Not only through doctrinal teaching and training
- But also through the imparting of spiritual life

This is a multiplication process rather than addition as most people may think. While the faithful men and women are in turn teaching others also; and you like Timothy are to raise up more faithful men and women – who shall be able to teach others also. This is the Lord's plan for reproducing ourselves through the power of the Gospel of Christ. Thus fulfilling Christ's commission using every saved person. He is LORD!

A spiritual creation

Earlier I spoke of our giving the Lord our total commitment [we have given ourselves away]. Is that impossible to do? Certainly as seen in the [*physical realm*], which is tinted with sin. God's plan kept secret from the foundation of the world was a new *spiritual creation*, *"one new man"* manifested in the physical realm The Scripture says,

> *"Having abolished in His flesh the enmity, that is, the law of the commandments contained in ordinances, so as to create in Himself one new man from the two, thus making peace, and that He may reconcile them both to God in one body through the cross, thereby*

putting to death the enmity" (Ephesians 2:15-16). Emphasis added throughout.

Paul was not saying that God had rejected the righteous standards of the law. Rather, in Christ the righteous standards that people could not reach have been accomplished. He is our righteousness and in Him believers fulfill the law. The Christian church, composed of both Jews and Gentiles is described as "one new man." In the early days of Christianity, the church was made up mostly of Jews. However, under the direction of the Holy Spirit, the believers witnessed to Gentiles, who soon came to outnumber them in the church (see Acts 10).

The Manifold Wisdom of God

The continuing incarnation of Jesus in His spiritual creation, the church, is related to God's plans for the world. Through His church, God intends the "manifold wisdom of God" be made known, not only on earth, but "to the rulers and authorities in the heavenly realm" (Ephesians 3:10).

His complex and manifold plan to redeem humankind and to glorify Himself is being worked out in the church that exists in a sin-warped world. Although humanity tries in every generation to modify God's plan to make it more palatable for them. His mandate concerning what we are to be and to do in carrying out His mandate still stands and reflects His will. In *A Theology of Church Leadership,* Lawrence O. Richards and Clyde Hoeldtke drives home Christ's continued expectancy of His witnesses today:

"You shall be My witness" Jesus said, as He explained His mission for the disciples (Acts 1:8). Worldwide witness is not only verbal, but it also includes total lifestyle change; it is not only individual, but is also a function of the Christian Community. *"All men shall know that you are My disciples,"* Jesus said in John 13, *"If you have love for one another."*

1. The witness to Jesus is the power of the gospel which brings many to a personal faith relationship with Christ. As the message is shared, God acts in the hearts of hearers, as He did in the early church (Acts 2:41).

2. The church has a special obligation to meet the physical as well as the spiritual needs of its members and to aid those outside (see James 2; 2 Corinthians 8 and 9).
3. Jesus saw worship as intrinsic to the life of believers in God: "The Father seeks such to worship Him" (John 4:23).
4. God acted in Christ to "purify for Himself a people who are His very own, eager to do good works" (Titus 2:14). This commitment is to be a central element in the life of God's people.[2]

Our hope will dazzle those in the world around us, so we should "always be prepared to give the reason for the hope that we have [in Christ]" (see 1 Peter 3:15).

Ministry of Reconciliation

The Apostle Paul, to whom the mystery of the church was revealed after having been kept secret in God from the foundation of the world, informs Christians that their mission involves "reconciliation" which means to change or restore thoroughly. The idea of two people who had something between them is restored:

- Bringing people into harmony with God through Christ and also bringing them into harmony with one another. Men are said to be enemies of God, because of sin (study Romans 5:6, 8, 10).
- Here is the mystery of God's great love or reconciliation. He did not reconcile and save us when we were righteous and good. He reconciled and saved us when we were enemies, ignoring and rejecting Him. It is because we are sinners and enemies that we need to be reconciled.

Reconciled

The way a person is reconciled to God is by the death of His Son, Jesus Christ. Very simply stated, when a person believes that Jesus Christ died for him or her:

- God accepts the death of Jesus Christ for the death of that person.
- God accepts the sins borne by Christ as the sins committed by the person.
- God accepts the condemnation borne by Christ as the condemnation due to the person.

Therefore, the person is freed from his or her sins and the punishment due for sins committed. It bears repeating! Christ bore both the sins and the punishment for that person. The person who truly believes that God loves that much – enough to give His only forgotten Son – becomes acceptable to God, and reconciled forever:

- God is the One who reconciles – not people.
- No individual can reconcile themselves to God; they cannot do enough work or enough good to become acceptable to God.
- All men can be reconciled to one another and brought together, if they look up to God through our Lord and Savior, Jesus Christ.
- People learn about reconciliation by the preaching of Jesus Christ.

"Now all things are of God, who has reconciled us to Himself through Jesus Christ, and has given us the ministry of reconciliation (2 Corinthians 5:18).

Christ was the first to preach the message. His followers are to follow in His path, for there's no other way that they can know that they can be reconciled to God apart from preaching.

"I am the door:
by Me
if any man enter in,
he shall be saved, and shall go in and out,
and find pasture" (John 10:9).

Access to the presence of God

> *"Having therefore, brethren, boldness to enter into the Holiest by the blood of Jesus"* (Hebrews 10:19).

Unlike the Israelites, who approached God at Mount Sinai with fear and trembling (see Exodus 20:16-21). Unlike the office of the President of the United States wherein our chances of entering in our lifetime is zero. Believers can approach God with boldness, because we possess Christ's righteousness and not our own (see Hebrews 10:35).

> *"Now then, we are ambassadors for Christ, as though God were pleading through us: we implore you on Christ's behalf, be reconciled to God"* (see 2 Corinthians 5:19).

Paul was an ambassador for Christ! His message was one of peace! God had paid the price for sin; God was not at war with sinners; sinners could now believe and be saved. What a tremendous message! The message for the church today is one of reconciliation: God in Christ on the cross has reconciled the world to Himself and is willing to save all who will trust His Son. Our message is not one of social reform although the gospel reforms lives (see Titus 2:11-15); ours is a message of regeneration. We represent Christ as we invite the lost to receive Him. What a privilege! As stated in an earlier section; all believers are ambassadors, whether we accept the commission or not.

> *"As the Father has sent me, also I send you,"* said Christ in (John 20:21).

A Counterculture

Scripture says that we have been rescued from Satan's kingdom and translated into the kingdom of God's dear Son (see Colossians 1:13). In His kingdom, there is a whole new way of life to learn and live. The church becomes the context in which Christians learn to live God's way. As a counterculture, the church demonstrates God's alternative lifestyle to the world. God's plan has many other aspects:

- The church has the mission of discipling and disciplining believers.
- The church is to "look after orphans and widows in their distress" (James 1:27).
- The church is to have a deep concern for the poor and the oppressed.
- The church is to bring healing – both inner healing and physical healing.

The Church on Purpose

God's purposes for His church are almost limitless! In complex and manifold ways, God's wisdom and power are demonstrated to all beings in the world through the church. But the greatest wonder of all is that:

- By the Spirit in us Jesus Himself walks the world.
- By the Spirit in us Jesus speaks the Good News.
- By the Spirit in us Jesus clothes the fatherless and feeds the hungry. (In those who are destitute Jesus also receives the gifts of clothing and food that are given in His name).
- By the Spirit in us Jesus exalts the Father in prayer and worship.
- By the Spirit in us Jesus continues to do good works.
- By the Spirit in us Jesus, who knew a joy untouched by circumstances, brings hope to the hopeless.
- By the Spirit in us Jesus reveals the Father and brings glory to God.
- By the Spirit in us Jesus reveals a positive and attractive holiness that exposes the darkness of sin.
- By the Spirit in us Jesus continues to show God's deep concern for justice.
- By the Spirit in us Jesus' reconciling touch is felt wherever there is division and pain.
- By the Spirit in us Jesus takes His firm stand against the powers of evil.
- By the Spirit in us Jesus is shaping a new lifestyle, a kingdom of God, a beachhead of the divine rule in the world of men.
- By the Spirit in us Jesus, the great physician, bends low to heal. In our flesh our Lord Jesus takes contemporary shape and form.

Christ in the Body

The vision of Jesus active in the body of Christ through the Holy Spirit in world missions is exciting. Wherever members of His body come in contact with the world; there He is present in them. Therefore, He is able to respond to any need through us. God's plan for His "spiritual creation" can only be effectively carried out through born again, yielded believers. Those who acknowledge and actively receive the presence, enablement and purpose of the divine love of God and the Spirit of God at work in their hearts:

- Through receiving true doctrinal teaching and training, [you] come into knowing and experiencing God, which makes you a true disciple of Christ.
- Through knowing and experiencing God as a true disciple [you begin to teach true doctrine and train others who become faithful disciples of Christ and teach others.
- Thus, the incorruptible Seed, the Word of God continues to reproduce itself in others until our Lord returns.

The Great Commandment

The discussion above shows just how important receiving and obeying the Great Commandment is to the true disciple of Christ. Jesus said,

> *"You shall love the LORD your God with all your heart, with all your soul, and with all your mind.* This is the first and great commandment. And the second is like it: *'You shall love your neighbor as yourself.'* On these two commandments hang all the Law and the Prophets" (Matthew 22:37-40).

Love God

The great commandment encompasses the entire faculties and at the same time underscores the completeness of the kind of love that is called for *[agape, unconditional love]*. In the second, the believers are prompted to measure their love for others, by how they desire others to love them.

This is the same idea as that of the Golden Rule. Jesus summarizes man's whole moral duty under two categories: love God and love your neighbors.

Truly this is the heart of discipleship. It is a known fact, no one can love God without knowing Jesus Christ as Savior (see John 8:42). And when you know and love God, the love of God will be shared with others (Romans 5:5)

Love your neighbor

People try to make the regeneration process so simple. The person is asked to repeat a few phrases or words – after which the person is welcomed to the body of Christ. For too many, that is the extent of their salvation experience. Without the "teaching of all things" as Jesus commanded, this person has actually been done a great injustice. Many come into the salvation experience with a lot of access baggage in their psyche and needing deliverance by the truth of God's Word.

Soon they find themselves in a Bible study and the subject is, "Love your neighbor as yourself." The problem with many is they really don't love themselves. Many times abuse, rejection, bullying [any age group] or any number of other negative behaviors by parents, mates, fellow workers, or circumstances toward them has forced his or her esteem below ground zero. Until we experiences proper self-love – we will never love outside of ourselves as long as the storms rage within. We need deliverance! We can't give to others what we refuse to accept for ourselves.

We can have personal peace because God loves us. John 3:16 is said to be the most beloved verse in the Bible. Only heaven knows the number of people saved through this one verse. We are a new spiritual creation in Christ Jesus; the old has passed away [bury it!] and the new has come (see 2 Corinthians 5:17). We need extensive teaching and training on loving ourselves. The Scripture informs that God created us in His own image, for His purposes, and for His glory.

Love yourself

Therefore, to love ourselves as God loves us means we seek His best for our lives according to His Word:

- We are transformed to His expectation [the image of His Son] – Romans 12:1-2.
- We live in obedience to His Word [His guidelines] – John 14:12-23.
- Overtime we learn to yield our whole person to the control, formation, and leading of the Holy Spirit – John 16:13-14.

When we do that, we begin to live as functional disciples (see Hebrews 5:14), instead of dysfunctional wavering individuals. The Holy Spirit is able to build the character of Christ, which is the fruit of the Spirit into our lives (Galatians 5:22-23).

The character of Christ (Fruit of the Spirit)

Character refers to our walk or lifestyles, our habits of living and thinking that manifests truly who we are (see Luke 1:6; Ephesians 4:17; 1 John 1:7). Our character also expresses daily conduct and behavior, since every Christian is indwelt by the Holy Spirit, who has shed the love of God in our hearts, therefore, we will manifest the fruit they produce in our lives:

> *"But the fruit of the Spirit is love, joy, peace, longsuffering, kindness, goodness, faithfulness, gentleness, self-control. Against such there is no law. And those who are Christ's have crucified the flesh with its passions and desires. If we live in the Spirit, let us also walk in the Spirit"* (Galatians 5:22-23).

The "fruit of the Spirit" are godly attitudes that characterize the lives of only those who truly belong to God by faith in Jesus Christ and are indwelt by the Spirit of God. The fruit produced by the Spirit consists of nine Christ-like characteristics commanded of the true Christian throughout the New Testament:

Character as an inward state

1. Love – The Greek term *"agape"* is the,love of choice, referring not to emotional affection, physical attraction, or a familial bond,

but to respect, devotion, and affection that leads to willing, self-sacrificial service (see John 15:13; Romans 5:8; John 3:16-17).

2. Joy – is happiness based on unchanging divine promises and kingdom realities. It is the sense of well-being experienced by one who knows all is well in his or her relationship with God. That is joy in spite of favorable or non-favorable life circumstances (see John 16:20-22).

3. Peace – is the inner calm that results from confidence in one's saving relationship with Christ. Like joy, peace is not related to one's circumstances of life (see John 14:27; Romans 8:28; and Philippians 4:6-7,9).

Character in expression toward others

4. Longsuffering – refers to the ability to endure injuries inflicted by others and the willingness to accept irritating or painful people and situations (see Ephesians 4:2; Colossians 3:12; 1 Timothy 1:15-16).

5. Kindness – is tender concern for others, reflected in a desire to treat others gently, just as the Lord treats all true Christians (see Matthew 11:28-29; 19:13-14; 2 Timothy 2:24).

6. Goodness – is moral and spiritual excellence manifested in active kindness (see Romans 5:7; 6:10; 2 Thessalonians 1:11).

Character of expression toward God

7. Faithfulness – is loyalty and trustworthiness (see Lamentations 3:22; Philippians 2:7-9; 1 Thessalonians 5:24; Revelation 2:10).

8. Gentleness – also translated "meekness" is a humble and gentle attitude that is patiently submissive in every offense, while having no desire for revenge or retribution.

9. Self-control – is the restraining of passions and appetites (see 1 Corinthians 9:25; 2 Peter 1:5-6).

This moral portrait of Christ is expected as a result of the believer's union with Christ and is a definition of "fruit" in John 15:1-8; while staying focused on Christ's finished work on the cross. This is wholly the fruit of the Spirit developed by Him in those believers who are yielded to Him (study John 15:15; 1 Corinthians 12:12, 13; Galatians 5:22, 23). This is the Christlikeness that God expects the Holy Spirit to form in every Christian, and our part is to yield to Him.

Love is the Greatest

The various purposes in the gift of the Holy Spirit's pouring the divine love within the disciple's heart are of unique importance. Without the Spirit's influence of divine love in the believer's heart, all other actions [i.e. your witness or gifts] that may be produced lose their true significance, thus failing to accomplish their true purposes. The Apostle Paul emphasizes the extreme importance of God's kind of love [*agape*]:

> *"Though I speak with the tongues of men and of angel, but have not love, I have become as sounding brass or a clanging symbol.*
>
> *And though I have the gift of prophecy, and understand all mysteries and all knowledge,*
>
> *And though I have all faith, so that I could remove mountains, but have not love, I am nothing"* Emphasis is mine.
>
> – 1 Corinthians 13:1-2

Paul puts himself in the place of a believer who exercises spiritual gifts but lack divine love [agape]. In Chapter 12, Paul elaborates on nine gifts of the Holy Spirit. He says to exercise the gift of tongues on such a high supernatural level that he speaks even the language of angels. He says that if he was to do this without divine love [agape], he would be absolutely nothing.

This applies equally to all the spiritual gifts. To use any of the gifts apart from divine love is to miss the whole purpose of the Holy Spirit's giving them. Then in chapter 14, Paul gives instructions on the proper operation of the gifts. In Romans 12:5, he cautions us to not think more highly of ourselves then we ought to think. In verse 13:1, it is possible that we have such a case. Notice the phrase *"I have become."* Undoubtedly there has been a change in this person.

The believer is not in the same spiritual condition as he or she was when originally baptized in the Holy Spirit. At the time the person has retained the outward manifestation but through disobedience or some other sin has not retained the inward condition of holiness or yielding to the Spirit. For those who might think this condition cannot happen?

Our unredeemed humanness (the flesh)

In an earlier section I said that a sinner has an appetite only for sin. But the Christian can not only live a holy life he or she can sin through the flesh, but not at the same time. The flesh opposes the work of the Spirit in us and leads the Christian toward sinful conduct and behavior that he or she would not otherwise be compelled to do (see Romans 7:14-25). The flesh is not simply the physical body, but includes the mind, will, and emotions which are all subject to sin. In general it refers to our unredeemed humanness; which is understandable and acceptable in the culture and society, but don't you falter or be misled by them!

We have a choice be led by the Spirit or by the flesh. Again, they are mutually exclusive (see Galatians 5:17). So either you live by the power of the Holy Spirit which results in righteous behavior and Christlike character [the fruit of the Spirit] or by the flesh which can only produce unrighteous behavior and attitudes [the works of the flesh].

Paul lists these works of the flesh in Galatians 5:19-21; the list is not exhaustive, encompassing three areas of human life: sex, religion, and human relationships – the works of the flesh are evident:

1. Adultery – unlawful sexual relations between men and women, single or married (v, 19).
2. Fornication – refers to all illicit sexual activity, including [but not limited to] adultery, premarital sex, homosexuality, bestiality, incest and prostitution (v. 19).
3. Lewdness – refers to lack of restraint associated with excessive sexual behavior and other sinful indulgencies (v. 19).
4. Uncleaness – includes whatever is opposite of purity and all sexual perversion (v. 19).
5. Idolatry – image worship; or anything on which affections are passionately set (v. 20).
6. Sorcery – witchcraft or practice of dealing with evil spirits, magical incantations, casting spells and charms upon one by drugs and portions of various kinds (v. 20).

7. Hatred – bitter dislike, abhorrence malice and all ill against another (v. 20).
8. Contentions – payback in kind the wrongs one to one (v. 20).
9. Jealousies – envy, striving to excel at the expense of others; evil attitude toward someone else (v. 20).
10. Outbursts of wrath – turbulent passions; rage and lasting anger (v. 20).
11. Selfish ambitions – excelling over others by any means (v. 20).
12. Dissensions – quarreling, disputes, stirring up grief and debating (v. 20).
13. Heresies – refers to a doctrinal view; a belief at variance with the recognized and accepted tenets of a system, church or party (v. 20).
14. Envy – jealousies, strife (v. 21).
15. Murders – to kill; to spoil or mar the happiness of another; hatred (v. 21).
16. Drunkenness – living intoxicated; slave to drink (v. 21).
17. Revelries – rioting (v. 21).

Paul concludes saying "and the like." He goes on to say, "Those who practice [*continual, habitual*] such things will not inherit the kingdom of God. *Practice* is the key word in Paul's warning. Because of these sins being practiced openly in much of the church today, it is not easy to distinguish one from the other.

Although Christians undoubtedly can fall into or commit these sins – these people whose basic character is summed up in the uninterrupted and unrepentant practice of them cannot belong to God (see 1 Corinthians 6:11; 1 John 3:4-10). The question often arises, "How can God use such a person in His service?"

Once a gift is given control passes from the giver to the receiver and therefore remains under the receiver. Whether he or she abuses or uses the gift – it is not taken away, control remains with the receiver. The Scripture says, "For the gifts and calling of God are irrevocable" (Romans 11:29). God will not take the gift back once He has given it to someone.

This means the responsibility to properly use the gift belongs to the receiver and not with God. This principle holds true not with spiritual gifts only; but in all areas of the Christian's life. In his book, *Foundational Truths for Christian Living,"* Derek Prince lists eight important results that

God desires to produce in the life of each individual believer (disciple) through the Baptism in the Holy Spirit:

1. Power to witness
2. Glorification of Christ
3. A gateway to the supernatural
4. Spirit empowered prayer
5. Revelation of the Scriptures
6. Daily Guidance
7. Impartation of life and health to the believer's body
8. Outpouring of divine love [agape] into the believer's life[3]

In the measure that we are filled with the Holy Spirit, is the same measure we shall be filled with divine love. We are not more filled with the Holy Spirit than we are filled with divine love. John applies the test in simple terms:

> *"No one has seen God at any time. If we love one another, God abides in us, and His love has been perfected in us. By this we know that we abide in Him, and He in us .... God is love, and he who abides in love abides in God, and God in him"* (1 John 4:12-13, 16).

Likewise, Paul assigns love to a place of unique honor among all God's gifts and graces:

> *"And now abide faith, hope, love, these three, but the greatest of these is love"* (1 Corinthians 13:13)

STUDY SUMMARY: CHAPTER 1

1. Christ's vision for us to reach the world is through _____ disciples.

2. We are to commit to others not only what we know: also what _____ _____.

3. In Romans 5:5, Paul says, "The love of God has been poured into our hearts. The Greek word for this kind of love is _____.

4. The verb form of the Greek word for love is _____.

5. Peter directly connects the possibility of Christians manifesting the divine love with the fact that they have been _____ _____.

6. The Great Commandment is the _____ of discipleship.

7. John 8:42 says, no one can love God without knowing _____ _____ as _____.

8. Without the "_____ _____ _____ _____" as Jesus commanded the Christian has been done an injustice.

9. The Scripture informs that God created us in His own _____.

10. The Holy Spirit builds the character of Christ, which is the fruit _____ ____ _____.

11. Based on our identity in Christ and our being conformed to His image by the Holy Spirit, we are becoming _____.

12. Romans 11:29 says, "The gifts and callings of God are _____."

13. In the same measure we are filled with the Holy Spirit, is the same measure we shall be filled with _____ _____.

14. Explain the love test in the space below:

15. _____ has been assigned a unique place of honor among all of God's gifts and graces.

·············· **CHAPTER 2** ··············

SO YOU DESIRE TO
BE A DISCIPLE

"Beloved, if God so loved us, we also ought to love one another"
(1 John 4:11).

I
n chapter one, we explored the [agape] love of God. God first loved us and He empowers us to love Him in return – then we can love ourselves. As we now look through our renewed eyes of love at the people around us, we see them differently than before. Now that we have received the love of God in our hearts, we are empowered to love and we desire to love "one another." The New Testament lists some sixty-one what I call, "one another" relational ministries.

We read for example that we are to love one another, to encourage one another, to forgive one another, and to exhort one another. On His last night, Jesus urged His disciples to carry this love (*agape*) forward. He repeats the commandment (see John 15:12-13) and exhorts His disciples [and us] to imitate Him in our love for one another. He is saying, "I have shown you My love, now you follow My lead." He made clear that His true disciples are identified by their love.

Later Peter wrote, "Above all things have fervent love for one another, for love will cover a multitude of sins" (1 Peter 4:8). He learned the truth of this verse while warming by the wrong fire. In a moment of fear, he denied that he ever knew Jesus. The love of God [agape] was really driven home with him when Jesus later sought him out and forgave him.

John was also inspired concerning the love of God. He reiterated the commandment on two occasions in 1 John 3: 11, 23), He added in chapter 4,

> *"If God so loved us, we ought to love one another. No one has seen God at any time. If we love one another, God abides in us, and His love has been perfected in us"* (vv. 11-12).

Christ loved Sinners

Hopefully we have established in our "knower" the truth that without the love of God [agape] in our hearts – we cannot be Christ's disciples. If we are to follow Jesus as His disciples we should live by the same values and priorities that He lived by. If we do then for us, being His disciples becomes our very life.

Religiosity

Not unlike Jesus' day, it is widely accepted among the religious folks that religious activity is the way to please God. Jesus was totally concerned with God and people. His lifestyle emerged out of simply loving God, our neighbors, and ourselves. Certainly His lifestyle in no way promotes a super sainthood. We sometime hear someone say, "The ground is level at the cross."

They are saying, "Christ loved sinners." There were no little insignificant people, nor hierarchy with Jesus (see Mark 10:42-45). He exclaimed,

> *"The Son of man came not to be ministered to, but to minister and give His life for many"* (v. 45). Study very thoroughly John 13:1-20. Christ is our Example:

- He identified with the unimportant, the weak, and the powerless.

- At His resurrection the first person to whom He appeared was a woman, the most powerless person in His culture.
- Bartimaeus was a blind insignificant beggar to everyone except Jesus (see Matthew 10:26-52).
- Jesus took time out to talk to children and to hold them on His knee (see Mark 10:13-16).
- To Jesus any person was very important.
- Jesus personified the biblical principle that life is relationships (see Genesis 2:18).

Jesus emphasized and demonstrated throughout His earthly ministry a life bearing the mark of profound love [agape]. As His disciples, we are commanded to do the same! We are to become like our Teacher.

The Dynamic Disciple

As dynamic disciples, the challenge to you and me today is to present the true gospel of Christ to people in a way that people can understand and accept. To do this we:

- Must "continue in the Word" and develop a healthy relationship with Christ.
- Must be sanctified (set apart from the world and set apart unto the Lord), and full of the Holy Spirit (see John 17:17; 14:13-15; Ephesians 5:18.
- Must be teachable and seeking first the kingdom of God (see 2 Peter 1:2-4; Matthew 6:33).
- Must develop human discipline with God's grace (see Philippians 2:12-13).
- Must realize that discipleship has a growth process.
- Must be developed in spiritual disciplines (2 Timothy 2:15).
- Must possess a deep love for God and others (see Matthew 22:37).
- Must have a daily diet of personal Bible study, prayer and meditation – submitting to the kingdom of God as the Spirit forms the inner man (see Psalm 119:173-175; Matthew 6:9-13, 33).

- Must submit to God's will in service daily to develop the outer man (see Romans 12:1-2).
- Must have a commitment to corporate worship, and counsel (see Hebrews 10:25).
- Must have a heart knowledge of right doctrine with conviction (see John 8:32).
- Must have a rich knowledge of the Word of God with a personal application (see Psalm 119:10-11; Proverbs 3:5-6; 2 Timothy 2:14-17).[4]

Discipleship and Commitment

> Jesus said, *"Come unto Me, all you who labor and are heavy laden, and I will give you rest. Take My yoke upon you and learn from Me, for I am gentle and lowly in heart, and you will find rest for your souls. For My yoke is easy and My burden is light"* (Matthew 11:28-30).

In his book, *The Complete Disciple,* Paul W. Powell says of this passage that Jesus used two great symbols for Christian commitment. The first is a cross. The second is a yoke. The cross and the yoke symbolize the two aspects of commitment. He offers the cross is an instrument of death; the yoke is the symbol of service. The cross suggests blood and the yoke suggests sweat.

As disciples, our commitment means we are ready for either death or service.[5] I stated in an earlier section when I joined the army as a career; that commitment required:

- Surrender to Uncle Sam
- Ready to die for our country
- Ready to work for him
- Ready to bleed or to sweat

Today many are settling for a religion wherein their practice is effective only in peace time; when the going gets rough they drop out or change their allegiance to that of the enemy. Christianity is a life in the kingdom of God; where Jesus is Lord! Being a disciple means that we are fully committed to our Lord for life in this world and in the eternal. Our commitment to Christ requires:

- Absolute surrender of all to Him
- Already died to self for Him
- Ready to work for Him
- Ready to suffer for Him
- Ready to bleed or sweat for Him; whichever He may require

Jesus spoke of the cross when He said, *"Whosoever will come after Me, let him deny himself, and take up his [or her] cross, and follow Me"* (Mark 8:34). When He spoke of the yoke He said, *"Take My yoke upon you, and learn of Me"* (Matthew 11:29). Anyone who is unwilling to deny him or herself cannot legitimately claim to be a disciple of Jesus Christ.

To Jesus, discipleship was following Him, not just His principles, ideas, or philosophy. Discipleship to Jesus was a concrete *relationship* with Him; which would result in "knowing Him." So knowing Christ requires intimacy, in this relationship there will be a conception and later a birthing of your maturity and your ministry of making disciples through reproducing yourself in others – who in turn will win still others (see 2 Timothy 2:2).

Making disciples is so important to Christ that a *crown of rejoicing* has been laid up for those who are faithful in this service. Love [agape] and commitment are characteristic of Christ's expectations for a dynamic disciple.

STUDY SUMMARY: CHAPTER 2

1. God first loved us and He empowers us to _____ _____ in return, then we can love _____.

2. What is the significance of the "one another" statements in the New Testament?

3. In _____, Peter said, "Above all things have _____ _____ for one another, for _____ will cover a multitude of sin."

4. Today many people accept religious activity as a way to _____ _____.

5. Christ saw no person as little and _____.

6. At His resurrection the first person to whom Christ appeared was a _____.

7. Christ commanded that we continue in the _____ and develop a healthy relationship with Christ.

8. 2 Timothy 2:15 says the disciple must be developed in spiritual _____.

9. The disciple must be sanctified and full of the _____ _____.

10. The disciple must be _____ and seeking first _____ _____ _____ _____ (see 2 Peter 1:2-4; Matthew 6:33).

11. The disciple must submit to God's _____ in service daily.

12. He or she must have a rich knowledge of the _____ _____ _____.

13. As disciples our commitment means we are ready for either a _____ or a _____.

14. When Jesus spoke of the cross He said, "_____" (see Mark 8:34).

15. When Jesus spoke of the yoke He said, "_____" (see Matthew 11:29).

CHAPTER 3

LEARN OF ME

"Take My yoke upon you, and learn of Me ...."
(Matthew 11:29).

In the Scripture, Jesus invites us to, "Learn of Me." Discipleship requires a "walking relationship" with Jesus Christ. This is an open invitation to all who will hear – "learn of Me." The only ones who will respond to the invitation are those who are burdened by their own spiritual deficiency and weariness of trying save themselves by keeping the law.

However, even this is not possible without a sovereignly bestowed spiritual awakening; all sinners refuse to acknowledge the depth of their spiritual lack. In verse 27, Jesus says that our salvation is the sovereign work of God.

Coming to Christ is a personal and decisive act. It is a choice that every person must make for themselves. The apostle Peter describes the genuine Christian as being, *born anew, not of perishable seed but imperishable, through the living and abiding word of God"* (1 Peter 1:23). The sons of the devil are the false Christians, who were never born again through faith in the finished work of Jesus Christ. But lay claim to being Christians because:

- They continuously fulfill some outward religious ritual.
- They have joined a local church.
- They rely on some outward conduct and performance.
- Like their father, the devil, they cover their own evil and sin in a false righteousness.

While they are indistinguishable to other people and even themselves; God knows they are the children of the devil. Planted by the devil to:

- Oppose the Word of God
- Snatch the Word from your heart
- Be alongside the righteous
- Present a plastic righteousness

Failure to adhere to this biblical picture as presented by Christ Himself in the parable of the wheat and the tares – will cause even some of those who love the church to be confused. The true disciples must be able to distinguish the dual, "true and false" nature of the church. Thus, we have two churches in one and must govern ourselves accordingly.

The confusion is inevitable unless this truth is well taught. Therefore, bickering and division are causing many local churches to forfeit their identity and mission to make disciples. It seems that too many of the local churches in America have for the most part forgotten who they really are.

Two-in-one Christians

In his book *"Body Life,"* Ray C. Stedman states that the division between true church and counterfeit church does not lie along denominational lines. True Christianity is not a matter of organizations or groups. We examine the lives of individuals whom we think manifest the counterfeit Christianity and those who manifest true Christianity and conclude that the matter is settled merely by our physical observations and resulting opinions. Stedman further expresses the fallacy in this thinking.

Therefore, genuine Christians can through spiritual ignorance or willful disobedience, display a false and counterfeit Christianity in their lives. Both of these pose the greatest hindrance to our experiencing the same power today as the church that turned the world upside down in the book of Acts.[6]

Many local churches across America have added fuel to the fire by reversing their concept of ministry from "be saved and belong" to "belong and be saved." That no doubt adds to the confusion, as this could easily mean accepting the unsaved into membership before they are actually saved. And if this unbiblical practice is not countered in a matter of time they can be assimilated right into the leadership positions of the church; many times due to some natural abilities or acquired skills.

Some true Christians continue to try separating the wheat and the tares even though they know what the Lord had to say concerning the matter (please study carefully Matthew 13:24-30). We need to be aware that elements of true and false Christianity will be intermingled in the same world, in the same church, even in the same person. Any attempt to weed out the false risks uprooting the true also.

Additionally, too often church leaders attempt to organize and institutionalize programs that work toward the achievement of one or more of the listed purposes of their mission in the world, simply because they continuously fail to hear what the Spirit is saying to the churches.

I once read an article concerning the treasury department's handling of counterfeit money. They burn it! It has absolutely no place in training new agents. The policy is to study and know the true money to a point that any counterfeit would automatically be spotted. Our task as Christ's disciples is similar. We must obey His way, will, and commands; as we learn of Him, which will strengthen the true wheat in the church to a point that the tares will be rendered powerless!

Otherwise, there is a tendency to try to organize people into work groups to meet needs or resolve problems. When church leaders set goals, make plans, and design programs they are no longer "body leaders" having taken on functions that in a living organism are decisions that belong to the head. The purposes of God for the body of Christ are achieved by the Head, Jesus Christ, incarnated through the Holy Spirit in us. The more Christians grow and mature into His likeness – the more His body [the church] will respond as He did to meet human needs and accomplish His mission in the world. The church should concentrate on the spiritual growth that brings members to maturity and Christlikeness, confident that Jesus will express Himself through them by the Spirit in them in a most powerful and unmistakable way. This is God's way and the only way Christians can touch the world around them as Jesus did.

Disciples or Spectators

Just as Christ left a specific word for our handling tares in the church; He left specific instructions through the apostle Paul concerning the church's work in the world. I stated in an earlier section, Christ commanded us to make disciples not converts or members. In order for the church to accomplish this, Paul wrote that apostles, prophets, evangelists, pastors, and teachers were given specifically to *"equip the saints for the work of ministry, for building up the body of Christ"* (study carefully Ephesians 4:12).

Over the years as a pastor, I ran into much resistance trying to implement this very passage in the churches to which I was called to pastor. Even with some open dissension and resistance, this is a responsibility that cannot be ignored – if the church is to be true to our Lord. I am pleased that more and more of our students have grasped these biblical truths and have put them into action.

This burden led my wife and me to establish the Bread of Life Bible Institute in 1998 to teach this biblical concept of ministry. We will not quite! Incorporated in this concept are development of the total fruit of the Spirit and the gifts of the Spirit; with each believer given at least one Spiritual gift by the Holy Spirit. Of course our message from the Lord in undertaking this ministry looked similar to that of the prophet Zechariah who was once confronted with a great mountain which God said would become a plain.

When Zechariah began to look around to see how this would happen and where the power would come from to level that mountain to a plain, the word of the Lord came to him: *"Not by might nor by power, but by My Spirit says the LORD, of hosts"* (Zechariah 4:6). Emphasis added.

As congregations dwindle, a great number of pastors and other church leaders are re-looking their concepts of doing church, many are finding that the church has drifted from the true model over the past centuries. Church history reports a great Holy Spirit restoration revival at the beginning of the twentieth century the 1906 Azusa Street revival in

Los Angeles; headed by an African American preacher named William J. Seymour.

This Holy Spirit restoration revival was ignored by many of the mainline denominational leaders for various reasons. However, the fruit of those decisions to ignore this mighty move of God has birthed a century of:

- Churches that lean to their own understanding through science and reason.
- Mix law with grace.
- Churches that substitute the non-spiritual programs, activities and format of the institutional church. Very few people are attracted to those non-relational fillers.

It has been said, "Because a thing has been practiced for a thousand years does not mean it is right. Likewise, because it has not been practiced for a thousand years does not make it wrong."

By My Spirit

This has been God's plan from the beginning. God sent Jesus from the spiritual realm in a physical body into the natural realm; and now through Him we can move from the physical realm to the spiritual realm in Christ Jesus. Thus, we are quickened by the Holy Spirit to the spiritual realm in regeneration, delivered from the kingdom of darkness to the kingdom of God's dear Son.

- The physically created world or realm created in the beginning will continue until the close of Jesus' millennial kingdom. At that time God will create a new universe, there will be the judgment of the fallen angels and the unsaved humans (study Revelation 20:11-15).
- Only those who are born twice, "born again," can escape this final judgment, also known as the second death.

Those who are born twice will die once – while those are born once will die twice. You must be born again! (see John 3:3).

Make it plain

It is necessary though we receive the Holy Spirit in the new birth, that we receive Him in His fullness, and through Him receive all the blessings promised. Acts 2:37-38 is the end of Peter's sermon on the Day of Pentecost, and it gives us a couple of essential conditions. Just as Peter concluded his message, so the church must teach very thoroughly the importance of repentance and the significant meaning of baptism. The people responded to Peter, "What shall we do?"

> *Then Peter said to them, "Repent and let everyone of you be baptized in the name of Jesus Christ for the remission of sins; and you shall receive the gift of the Holy Spirit."*

There we have the promise: *"You shall receive the gift of the Holy Spirit."* The conditions are clearly stated: *"Repent and be baptized."* To repent means to sincerely turn from all sinfulness and rebellion and totally submit ourselves without reservations to the Lord and to His will and commandments. To be baptized is to go through an ordinance whereby each of us is personally and visibly identify with Christ to the world in His death, burial, and resurrection (see Romans 6).

STUDY SUMMARY: CHAPTER 3

1. In Matthew 11:27 Jesus says, "Our salvation is the sovereign work of _____.

2. The sons of the devil are the false _____ who were never _____ _____.

3. Describe Peter's description of the genuine Christian in 1 Peter 1:23 below:

4. Children of the devil are indistinguishable to _____ _____ and even to _____.

5. From chapter 3 list three reasons Satan plants his children among the true Christians: 1) _____ 2) _____ 3) _____.

6. Confusion concerning the wheat and the tares is due to a lack of _____.

7. Counterfeit Christians can only manifest counterfeit Christianity. However, true Christians can manifest both true and false though not at the same time. (true or false).

8. Many local churches have changed their concept in the invitation from "be saved and belong" to "_____ and _____ _____."

9. The true wheat in the church may be strengthened to render tares powerless by obeying Christ's command to _____ of _____.

10. What were Jesus' instructions to His disciples concerning the handling of tares in the church and why?

11. Why did Paul say Christ placed apostles, prophets, evangelists, pastors, and teachers in the church?

12. God's answer to Zechariah was, "Not by might nor by power, but by _____ _____ says the Lord of hosts."

13. The 1906 Azusa Street revival was a major move of God in Los Angeles headed by an African American preacher. The movement was ignored by many mainline denominations. "What were the results as reported by this writer?" Explain below:

14. At the present time Christ is building a _____ creation.

15. The Christian church, composed of both Jews and Gentiles is described as _____ _____ _____.

SECTION II

CONTINUE IN MY WORD

CHAPTER 4

OUR HOPE OF GLORY

"Since we heard of your faith in Christ Jesus and of your love for all saints; because of the hope which is laid up for you in heaven, of which you heard before in the word of the truth of the gospel" (Colossians 1:4-5).

"Now hope does not disappoint, because the love of God has been poured out in our hearts by the Holy Spirit who was given to us" (Romans 5:5).

I n obedience to Christ's command the young church made disciples as they went about their daily living. What was their motivation? In the text above Paul points to several spiritual motivating factors that moved these believers. If we are going to have radical restoration in local churches today; our motivation must be the same factors that spiritually moved the disciples in the early church:

- The hope of glory
- The love of God [agape]
- The Holy Spirit

- The Word of God

Our hope of glory

The songwriter Albert A. Goodson wrote in his timeless hymn, *The solid Rock*, "My hope is built on nothing less, Than Jesus' blood and righteousness; I dare not trust the sweetest frame, But wholly lean on Jesus' name.
Refrain
On Christ, the solid rock, I stand – all other ground is sinking sand, All other ground is sinking sand.

The hope that believers have of their future glory with God will not disappoint them by being unfulfilled. They will not be put to shame or humiliated. God works the same today, as believers endure tribulation and rejection; the Spirit works in them to develop certain qualities and virtues that will strengthen them and draw them into a closer relationship with the Lord. The result is fortified hope in God and His promises for the final hour.

Christ had told His disciples that if the world hated Him they would hate His followers. If people persecuted Him they would persecute His followers also (see John 15:19-20).

The world could not understand the hope of Christ's followers which enabled many of them to stand persecution even unto death. In Colossians 1:26-27, God revealed to Paul the mystery that had been hidden from the ages and generations. The mystery is the *union of Jews and Gentiles in one body, Christ's church; therefore now Christ lives within Gentile believers also – Christ in you, the hope of glory.* Emphasis added.

Paul was warning the believers not to be taken in by any philosophy that does not conform to a proper knowledge of Jesus Christ. The false teachers at Colosse had combined worldly philosophies with the gospel. Our nation has been inundated with these philosophies of old. They have simply been repackaged or made over. Similarly secular humanists and atheists have done the same by embracing and repackaging many of the old secular philosophies. Claiming not to be a religion; its adherents foster a humanistic world view that does not believe that God or the supernatural exist.

As America becomes more secularized, this erroneous philosophy is spreading like wildfire, teaching that humanity is the measure of all things. The fool has said in his heart, "No God!" Their goal is to secularize and destroy America. They have wreaked havoc with many of our founding institutions. Are you alarmed? Notice some examples of their subtle work:

- Parents are systematically being removed as the primary persons in the welfare, education, and discipline of their children.
- Individualism and political correctness are subtly and systematically altering our biblical worldview.
- Secular factions are striving to remove Jesus' name from the public square.
- Secular federal judges are stamping out "we the people."
- Biblical marriage and the family are being systematically removed and destroyed by secularism.

I can remember back in my childhood days that "rat poison" was boldly marked with a scary skull and cross bones, along with and an enlarged "WARNING: POISON" meaning certain death!

Today the poisons [erroneous philosophies of old] have been repackaged, the name changed to DECON or some other catchy scientific title, the skull and cross bones have been removed, the poison is formed into pellets, and the kicker is no smelling of the "dead rat!" In the final analysis it's still the same old "rat poison" and it will kill if consumed by the rat or you!

The reason the disciples of Christ can have fortified hope and stand persecution in confidence is because they not only have a hope of glory, but also since "rebirth," had the assurance of the divine love of God poured out in our hearts and the Spirit given to us" (see Romans 5:5). Don't fool yourself into thinking you can stand in the natural!

The love of God poured out

Paul is not speaking of love produced by human effort, *eros* from which we get the word erotic or Hollywood's romantic style love. Neither is he speaking of *phileo,* love toward man, but he is speaking of *agape,* love of God – God's own divine love that the Holy Spirit pours out in the disciple's heart.[7] This enabling unconditional love of God is imparted by the Holy Spirit and is high as the heavens above any form of human love.

Love is a noun [agape] and love is a verb [agapeo]

The perfect love between the Persons of the Godhead, the Father, the Son and the Holy Spirit will help us to fully understand as the words of the Apostle John become a reality:

> *"Beloved, let us love one another, for love [agape] is of God; and everyone who loves [agapao] is born of God and knows God. He who does not love [agapao] does not know God, for God is love" [agape]* (1 John 4:7-8).

The manifestation of *agape* commences in the human experience with the new birth. This love comes only from God. John is in harmony with the words of Peter in 1 Peter 1:22-23:

> *"Since you have purified your souls in obeying the truth through the Spirit in sincere love for the brethren, love [agapao] one another fervently with a pure heart, having been born again, not of corruptible seed but incorruptible, through the Word of God which lives and abides forever."[8]*

Notice, when Peter says, *"Love one another fervently with a pure heart,"* the verb he uses for "love" is once again that for divine love [agapao]:

- Peter directly connects this possibility of Christians manifesting the divine love with the fact that they have been born again of the incorruptible Seed of God's Word.
- That is to say, the potentiality of divine love [agape] is contained within the divine seed of God's Word implanted in their hearts at the new birth. Each seed [Word] has within, the power to reproduce itself in others!

However, God intends for this initial experience of divine love, received at the new birth, to be immeasurably increased and expanded through the power of the Holy Spirit, the Spirit of Truth.

Your precise nature

In his letter to the Romans, Paul defines the precise nature of this divine love poured out within the believer by the Holy Spirit.

- He points out that even natural love without the grace of God might die for a friend if he or she was good and righteous. Mother or father my die for their child.
- He shows that the divine supernatural love of God is seen in the fact that Christ died for sinners, who could have no claims upon any kind of natural life whatever.

He uses three phrases in Romans 5:6-8 to describe the condition of those for whom Christ has died (1) "without strength" (2) "ungodly" and (3) "sinners." This means that those for whom Christ died were:

- At that time not able to help themselves
- Hopeless
- Totally alienated from God
- In open rebellion against God

The Apostle John defines divine love in a similar fashion:

> *"In this love [agape] of God was manifested toward us, that God has sent His only begotten Son into the world, that we might live through Him"* (1 John 4:9).

- This divine unconditional love does not depend upon anything worthy of love in which it is directed and it does not reciprocate before it gives all.
- It gives first and freely to those who are unlovable, unworthy, and even in open rebellion.

Characteristics of the Love of God [agape]

- **It suffers long** – is patient (1 Thessalonians 5:14).
- **It is kind** – is gentle especially with those who hurt (Ephesians 4:32).

- **It does not envy** – is not jealous of what others have (Proverbs 23:17).
- **It does not parade itself** – does not put itself on display (John 3:30).
- **It is not puffed up** – is not arrogant or proud (Galatians 6:3).
- **It does not act rudely** – is not mean-spirited, insulting others (Ecclesiastes 5:2).
- **It does not seek its own** – way, or act pushy (1 Corinthians 10:24).
- **It is not provoked** – or angered (Proverbs 19:11).
- **It thinks no evil** – does not keep score on others (Hebrews 10:17).
- **It rejoices not in iniquity** – takes no pleasure when others fall into sin (Mark 3:5).
- **It rejoices in the truth** – is joyful when righteousness prevails (2 John 4).
- **It bears all things** – handles the burdensome (Galatians 6:2).

Give yourself away

- Jesus our Savior and Example expressed the divine love [agape] in His prayer for those who were crucifying Him, *"Father forgive them, for they know not what they do"* (Luke 23:34).
- Stephen expressed divine agape [love] as he was being stoned to death; *"Lord do not charge them with this sin"* (see Acts 7:60). As Jesus had done – Stephen requested mercy for his killers!

Love [agape] continues in the age to come; it is eternal, complete and fulfilling. The Scriptures differentiates between being dependent upon God, or childlike; and being childish or immature (Matthew 16:3). All manifestations of the Spirit must at the same time manifest the ways of love – for love is the ultimate issue behind all things.

STUDY SUMMARY: CHAPTER 4

1. List four factors that motivated the early church?
   - _____
   - _____
   - _____
   - _____.

2. What did Christ have to say concerning the persecution of the saints in John 15:19-20?

3. Briefly explain the mystery of the ages covered in chapter 4 in the space below:

4. Secular humanism does not claim to be a _____ and therefore denies the existence of _____ and _____ _____.

5. The goal of secularists and atheists is to _____ America.

6. Briefly explain 2 Corinthians 5:17 in the space below:

7. What is the Greek word [noun] for the love of God? _____.

8. What is the Greek word [verb] for the love of God? _____.

9. Fill in: Now _____ does not disappoint, because the _____ of _____ has been _____ _____ in our hearts ....."

10. Peter connects the possibility of Christians manifesting the [agape] love in the _____ _____.

11. He said, they have been born again of the _____ _____.

12. The divine seed is the _____ of _____.

13. Paul uses three phrases to describe the conditions of those for whom Christ died 1) _____ 2) _____ 3) _____.

14. Divine love is _____ and does not depend upon anything _____ of love in which it is directed.

15. Divine love gives first and freely to those who are _____, _____, and even in _____ _____.

43

······················ CHAPTER 5 ······················

DON'T DIVORCE THE HOLY SPIRIT

"Now hope does not disappoint because God has poured the love of God into our hearts by the Holy Spirit who was given unto us" (Romans 5:5).

"You shall receive power after the Holy Spirit has come upon you" (Acts 1:8). Emphasis is mine throughout.

At times as we watch Christian television some of the ministers seem to be trying to convince the viewing audience that we have a handle on world witness for Christ, claiming extreme successes. Yet statistics reflect some 2 billion people who have never heard the saving gospel of Christ. Then there are increasing billions around the world assimilated into false religions; which unless countered will lead billions to eternal hell.

Meanwhile, back in our local churches many are setting goals for the season which equate to family vacations, camps, programs to support the budget of comfortable, entertainment and many other non-spiritual family oriented activities, at the same time kingdom-building outreach is not a consideration. Many churches never consider Christ's global commission: "Make disciples of all nations."

We know from Scriptures stated in previous chapters, that in the new birth God has given the believer the power of His Holy Spirit to enable him or her with other believers collectively to reach the whole world with the gospel of Christ. If we really believe God's Word and take a real honest look at the millions of people starving without food and clean water in the world around us; perhaps our missions priorities would change! There are ministries working hard striving to alleviate these problems. Often we look at the problem and do nothing because we think we are too small and our contribution won't make a difference. You should overcome that natural attitude and ask God to guide you to those ministries you should help, which are already in place doing the work. Today the Word of God admonishes us to "Hear what the Spirit is saying to the churches" (Revelation 2:7). "Are you listening?"

Don't divorce the Holy Spirit [The age of the Holy Spirit]

During this present age the Lord is building His Spiritual church; which the gates of hell shall not prevail against. He is accomplishing this by the Holy Spirit in all His glorious operations working through all who believe on the Father through the Son. At the same time too many local churches have divorced themselves from the Holy Spirit and the Spiritual church He is building, [the true Body of Christ].

Who is the Holy Spirit?

From the start, the Holy Spirit is not an impersonal force, or mere influence and certainly not an "it!" The Holy Spirit is the third divine person of the eternal Godhead, co-equal, co-eternal, and co-existent with the Father and the Son. It is His ministry to convict and convert people as well as to reveal the Son and the Father to the believer. Since the glorification of the Lord Jesus Christ, and Pentecost, God's eternal plan has been given over to the Holy Spirit. The Old Testament foretold the coming of *"the last days"* when the Holy Spirit would be poured out upon all flesh – in contrast to Old Testament times when He was only available to a small number in Israel. This is why the present era is known as the age of the Holy Spirit.

The Holy Spirit as a divine title seems harder for Christians to relate to than the titles "Father" and "Son" (see Matthew 28:19). These titles have a much more human feeling about them than "the Holy Spirit." But this does not deny the personality of the Spirit though invisible and incorporeal, for "God is a Spirit" (John 4:24) yet He is a real divine Person. Emphasis added throughout.

No Spirit – no power

Many churches have settled for their own non-spiritual belief systems and naturally-envisioned projects; while establishing mega-budgets maintained by time consuming programs and schemes. In His letters to Timothy, Paul warns that local churches in the last days will be characterized by **"no power"** and **"no spirit;"** which equates to [denial of the Holy Spirit's ministry in our individual lives and churches]. God gave Him to us [for His eternal purposes] and without Him we can do nothing of spiritual value – don't divorce Him!

We know that the New Testament never tells us to build a house for the Lord especially one that invites people to come to us. Instead it commands us to give ourselves away going to other people. We hear sermons admonishing us to go, Sunday school and small groups' studies say go, our own personal Bible study says go, but more importantly, Christ commanded that we "go and as we go make disciples … teaching them." But the occasional visitor to our churches convinces us that it's okay to stay put. The Bible admonishes us that to "know to do right and not do it, is sin." Is that why the world calls us hypocrites? Is that why millennials [young people ages 18-30] shy away from our local churches?

Many of our modern and contemporary churches have acquired an inward look [for comfort and entertainment] rather than an outward look [sacrifice and service] – as a result many people who left the traditional/ institutional churches for the more contemporary settings are leaving them claiming their spiritual needs are not being met there either.

> Research shows that the millennials [18 to 30 something's] are leaving those churches in search of a truly Christ-centered, Holy Spirit empowered, Bible- believing church for mentorship, authentic worship experience, and service (outside the walls).

Much of this non-spiritual focus has blurred or totally caused the loss of the important work of the Holy Spirit today – and the command to "make disciples" is totally replaced with programming which is strictly designed to support various activities geared to fill the pews and to support the maintenance requirements of the physical building. It's quite obvious that truth, love and the ministry of the Holy Spirit are missing in the fore-mentioned scenarios.

How did the church get here?

Either Christ is the Head of the church or there is no head! When a person is the head, the Godhead is denied. Human leadership depends on hierarchy and the law. The church of Jesus Christ is justified by the faith of Christ and not by works of the law (see Galatians 2:16). Please review this chapter while studying Section III on Headship.

The Ministry of the Holy Spirit

Although as a Man the Lord Jesus is in heaven. Remember the Holy Spirit was the source of power for Jesus' entire period of preaching and teaching on earth. He depended totally on the Holy Spirit. If Jesus depended totally upon the Holy Spirit in such a manner – how much more should His disciples constantly depend upon the Holy Spirit.

Jesus promised His disciples that when He had returned to heaven, He would send the Holy Spirit to take His place as His personal representative to be their Paraclete – Counselor, Comforter, or Helper ["the one called alongside to help them"].

In the believer

All that God has for us and wants to do in us will only be done by the operation of the Holy Spirit. The Lord Jesus is the pattern Son of God who is the example of the Holy Spirit's work in the human being in an unhindered operation. In spite of the many theories and opinions to the contrary, the children of God, as members of His church must follow in Jesus' steps submitting ourselves fully to the same work of the Holy Spirit.

Additionally, the Holy Spirit indwells the believer's spirit and guides him or her in all truth, as He produces Christ-likeness in character and fruit in the believer's life bringing about the resurrection and immortality to believers bodies in the last day (Galatians 5:22, 23; Romans 8:11; 1 Corinthians 15:47-51; 1 Thessalonians 4:15-18).

In the Church

Just as Jesus Christ, the Head of the body was under total control and domination of the Holy Spirit, and the Spirit was able to flow freely in perfect and unhindered operation; the same is manifested in the church of God as the visible and mystical body of Christ on earth. He formed the Church on the Day of Pentecost into a corporate structure, to be the new and living temple of God, setting believers into their places as living stones in the New Covenant temple (1 Corinthians 3:16; 16:16; Ephesians 2:20-22).

The Baptism of the Holy Spirit

The baptism of the Holy Spirit is an essential experience of divine love that God extends for every true believer to receive. That means that this one-time baptizing of the believer in the Holy Spirit is first of all an undisputable doctrinal truth. In His commission to His disciples Jesus promised,

> *"But you shall receive power when the Holy Spirit has come upon you; and you shall be witnesses to Me in Jerusalem, and in all Judea and Samaria, and to the end of the earth"* (Acts 1:8).

The apostles' [and our own] mission of spreading the gospel was and is the major reason for the baptism of the Holy Spirit. This event dramatically altered world history, and the empowered gospel message eventually reached all parts of the earth (Matthew 28:19, 20).

The apostles had already experienced the Holy Spirit's saving power. Soon they would receive in the baptism of the Holy Spirit a new dimension of power for witness and service. In order to understand this new dimension, we must learn all we can about the spiritual realm. The spiritual ream is actually more real than this physical realm.

In the New Testament, the spiritual realm is eternal and viewed as more than our heavenly home when we die. But as a present reality available to all believers who embrace the work and ministry of the Holy Spirit. As we observe the New Testament, we readily come to understand that humanity originates in another realm and has a destiny beyond this earth.

Notice, in 1 Corinthians 2:6-16, Paul speaks of wisdom and truth flowing out of the spiritual dimension into our present world. These revelations can only be received by an individual whose human spirit has been made alive by the baptism of the Holy Spirit (see 1 Corinthians 6-11):

- Believers can be taught by the Holy Spirit (1 Corinthians 2:13).
- Spiritual gifts are given by the Holy Spirit (1 Corinthians 2:12).

In the natural, human beings cannot receive the things of the Spirit of God (Corinthians 2:14). A person must be born again and have a renewed mind [a new way of thinking] taken over by the Holy Spirit. Thus, "the mind of Christ" takes over the life of the believer:

- These verses clearly indicate that we who are alive in Christ have access to that realm referred to in Ephesians 2:5-6 as "the heavenly places."
- This is the realm where Christ is presently enthroned at the "right hand" of the Father where He intercedes for us (Ephesians 1:20).
- The Holy Spirit also intercedes for us (see Romans 8:26, 34).
- True worship occurs in this realm and also victories of spiritual warfare are accomplished here (see Ephesians 6:12).
- It is the realm where the impossible becomes possible!

The Holy Spirit in the World

The work of the Holy Spirit is summarized in John 16:9-11. The Holy Spirit came with a three-fold ministry in relations to the world: 1) to reprove the world of sin, 2) of righteousness and, 3) of judgment:

1. **Of Sin** – because they believe not on Christ. The sin of unbelief is the root sin of all others. This area of reproof or conviction deals especially with the sin of man.
2. **Of Righteousness** – because Jesus Christ has gone to the Father and at present we do not see Him. This area of conviction involves the righteousness of Christ, as the Savior of men.
3. **Of Judgment** – because the prince of this world, Satan, was judged at Calvary. This area of conviction involves the judgment of Satan and His hosts and their defeat at Calvary.

I have attempted to show the relationship between the Lord's new spiritual creation [one new man] in Christ and the necessity of the Holy Spirit in the lives of the people of God.

STUDY SUMMARY: CHAPTER 5

1. Statistics reflect some _____ _____ people who have not heard the saving gospel of Christ.

2. Many local churches set _____ for family, vacation, camp programs etc. while kingdom _____ outreach is not considered.

3. The global commission says, "_____ _____ of all nations."

4. In the _____ _____, God has given each of us the _____ of His _____ _____.

5. During the church age the Lord is building His _____ church.

6. Paul said in the last days local churches will be characterized by no "_____" and no "_____."

7. Instead of inviting people in, the New Testament church is to _____ _____ _____ _____.

8. What essential ministry is lacking in most churches today?

9. Jesus promised He would send a paraclete which means _____, _____, or _____.

10. The Holy Spirit indwells the believer's _____.

11. The Spirit _____ to the believer (Acts 8:29).

12. The Spirit _____ the believers and guide them into _____.

13. The Spirit _____ life.

14. The Holy Spirit formed the _____ on the _____ of Pentecost.

15. The Lord Jesus is the _____ of the _____ in heaven and He directs His affairs through the _____ _____.

··········· **CHAPTER 6** ···········

CONTINUE IN MY WORD

"If you abide in Me, and My words abide in you, you will ask what you desire, and it will be done for you" (John 15:7).

I t is often said of Christians concerning the Word of God, "they know the Word – they just don't do the word." I believe, if local churches would truly expose their members to the truth of God's Word and teach a biblical worldview; the people would be more likely to obey it. That statement "they know it, but won't do it" is probably more a defensive excuse for an ineffective spiritual formation training strategy.

More than likely people with this thought are probably thinking from an intellectual point of view which indicates liberalism, pluralism and compromise on the part of many pastors and teachers. In most cases they do know – but have an inadequate experience with Jesus Christ! God's thinking is just the opposite of their thinking. This spiritual truth is especially true as we abide "in Christ."

Paul uses the phrase "in Christ" to speak of a Christian's legal and family position as a result of the grace of God. The emphasis is "in Me" in this passage. Jesus' purpose was to move His disciples from servants to friends. Notice:

> *"Greater love has no one than this, than to lay down one's life for his friends. You are My friends if you do whatever I command you. No longer do I call you servants for a servant does not know what his master is doing; but I have called you friends, for all things that I heard from My Father I have made known unto you. You did not choose Me, but I chose you and appointed you that you should go and bear fruit, and that your fruit should remain, that whatever you ask the Father in My name He may give you"* (John 15:13-16).

This would involve a process of discipline in regard to His commandments. It started with selection, moved to servanthood and grew friendship that you should go and bear fruit. Once the fruit is on the vine, the vinedresser cleanses the fruit of bugs and diseases. The spiritual counterpart is cleansing which is done through the Word of God.

For the branch to produce more fruit, it must abide, which means to dwell, to stay, to settle in, and sink deeper. The way to abide in Christ is to obey (see 15:10; 1 John 3:24). The Christian who lovingly obeys the Word of God produces much fruit. Apart from Christ, a Christian cannot accomplish anything of permanent spiritual value.

The Christian can do nothing of spiritual value apart from Christ!

To not abide in Christ brings serious consequences:

- The loss of fellowship
- The loss spiritual life
- The loss of reward

Follow then Know

This is vividly seen in Jesus' washing the disciples' feet. Not understanding, Peter said to Him, "Lord, are You washing my feet?" Jesus answered and said unto him, *"What I am doing you do not understand now, but you will know after this"* (John 13:6-7). Emphasis added.

Life and discipleship with Jesus are the only school for the understanding of heavenly things. So this passage of Scripture is actually a law of the Kingdom, especially true of daily cleansing of which it was first spoken concerning daily keeping.

The cleansing that Christ does at salvation never needs to be repeated – atonement is complete at this point. But all who have been cleansed by God's gracious justification [imputed righteousness] need constant washing [sanctification] in the experiential sense as they battle sin in the flesh (see Philippians 3:8, 9; 3:12-14) respectively.

In his book, *"Abide in Christ,"* Andrew Murray suggests several time-tested lessons in the school of God:

• Receive what you do not comprehend.
• Submit to what you can not understand.
• Accept and expect what to reason appears a mystery.
• Believe what looks impossible.[9]

If you abide in My Word, you shall understand the truth. In these and other words of Jesus we are taught that there is a required "renewed mind" and "transformed life" which must precede the understanding of truth. True discipleship consists in first following, and then knowing the Lord. Murray continues the only way to the full blessedness of knowing Christ.

• The believing surrender to Christ
• The submission to His Word
• Expect what appears most improbable[10]

Into Our Destinies

The previous guiding principles through the Holy Spirit within prepares us for the destiny God has prepared for us – without our always knowing how. In the face of this biblical truth, many of our Christian television personalities seem to lead people to believe that their spiritual destiny is determined the same secular way as the unsaved person in the natural would pursue [with no spirit]!

The Holy Spirit works in tandem with the Word of God. Therefore, the disciple on the strength of the Lord's many promises, coupled with our trusting in His faithfulness, yields to the leading of the Holy Spirit. It is important to note that true believers move by faith not necessarily clear to the intellect of what he or she is to do.

EXAMPLE IS THE BEST TEACHER!

And so the Word of God and the indwelling Holy Spirit are to the mature disciple sufficient guarantee that he or she will be taught of the Spirit to abide in Christ.

Faith trusts the working of the Holy Spirit unseen in the deep recesses of the true inner life.

The Spirit of Life

The Holy Spirit is the Spirit of life in Christ Jesus; and it is His work:

- To foster us
- To guide us
- To strengthen us, and
- To perfect the new life within us

And all in proportion as the disciples yield themselves in simple trust to the unseen Spirit of life working from the inside out. Then, coming through the heart and life into the understanding, the Spirit makes us know the truth – not as mere thought-truth, but as the truth which is in Christ Jesus. If you want the Holy Spirit to guide you into this abiding truth and life, your first need is to continue in the Word, and have faith not just personal faith, but be "faithful," "the faith once delivered to the saints" (see Jude 3).

Satanic deception

As in the early church, false teachers have sneaked into the local churches today exploiting their spiritual ignorance with pluralism and the secular worldview of no God and no supernatural openly challenging the Christian worldview in every quarter.

If you are a Christian and not studying God's Word to show yourself approved, you are opening yourself up for demonic activity including deception. The Apostle Paul admonishes:

> *"Now the Spirit expressly says that in latter times some will depart from the faith, giving heed to deceiving spirits and doctrines of demons speaking lies in hypocrisy, having their own consciences seared with a hot iron"* (1 Timothy 4:1, 2).

Popularity of the Bible

Many nominal or carnal Christians will do more harm than good trying to explain the Bible with their opinions, second-hand theology, and false doctrinal teaching:

- Others are standing away from "the faith" (see 1 Timothy 1:19-20).
- Many local churches are not teaching and promoting a biblical worldview (see Daniel 7:25; 8:23; Matthew 24:4-12).
- Many in the church are failing to walk obediently (see John 19:25-27).
- Many preachers and pastors are neglecting the power of the gospel, which provides the only means to life.
- Christ's sacrificial substitution for our sins through His death, burial and resurrection should be the motivating factor behind the way we conduct ourselves everywhere we go and everything we do.
- Only the power of the gospel, [hear and act on it] can set you free from sin.

- We are commanded to hear the gospel – many claim to have heard the gospel. The idea is to hear and take action; one without the other is incomplete [two acts in one movement].

Through the gospel, the Spirit clothes us with the righteousness of Christ, [Justification] and renews us, [regeneration], conforming us daily to the image of Christ [sanctification].

Discipline

Discipline in godliness affects both the present and future aspects of the Christian's life. The present aspects include:

- Loving the Lord with all of our heart and soul
- Loving others as we love ourselves
- Obedience
- Purpose
- Fruit of the Spirit

Remember! If your love relationship with God is not right, nothing else in life will be right. The apostle Peter has already assured us that God has given us all that you need for life and godliness (2 Peter 1:3).

Known by their fruit

Speaking of the Holy Spirit, Jesus said the Holy Spirit would come, lead, teach, and guide us into all truth. We know that the inner conflict between the flesh and the spirit is a living reality. Except our spirit be regenerated by the Holy Spirit to new life, we are dead. I can' understand why it is so hard for us to accept the fact that He is the Spirit of Life. I said earlier, He gives us life in the new birth. It is His empowerment and the Word of God that keeps us from falling.

The only consistent way to overcome the temptations of the flesh is to walk in the power of the Spirit. The Christian under the Spirit's guidance and control is assured of absolute victory over the sinful desires of the flesh. When the lusts of the flesh are free to operate in the Christian's life such behavior is positive proof that the person is not living under the power of the Holy Spirit (see vv. 16, 18,22, 23) but the "fruit" manifested proves the individual is being energized by Satan and his hosts (see Matthew 16:23; Acts 5:3).

Christians are spiritually crucified with Christ (see Galatians 2:20). Therefore, we no longer have to follow the values and desires of the world (see Galatians 6:14). Again, it is impossible to apply spiritual reality to the lusts of the flesh in your own natural power. In v. 16, the Apostle Paul exhorts the Christians to "walk in the Spirit" and he or she will not fulfill the lust of the flesh. He specifically informs us that the production of the fruit of the Spirit is done by the Holy Spirit Himself in the Christian's life.

In Romans 8:29, the Apostle Paul states that God desires that the character of each of his chosen children undergo a conformational process and become like His Son. Jesus' teaching on the vine, branches and a fruitful harvest serves as an appropriate analogy depicting the process. The expected end is one who has developed the same fruit that were easily recognizable in His life. Jesus said,

> *"I am the true vine, and My Father is the vinedresser. Every branch*
> *in Me that does not bear fruit He takes away; and every branch that*
> *bears fruit He prunes, that it may bear more fruit"* (John 15:1-2).

This involves a process of personal discipline in regard to Christ's commandments. No plant produces fruit instantly; fruit is the result of a process. That is also the case with Christians. Pruning coincides with "cleanses." Once the fruit appears on the vine, the vinedresser cleanses the fruit of bugs and disease. The spiritual comparison is the cleansing which is accomplished through the Word. Jesus said, "You are already clean because of the Word which I have spoken to you" (v. 3). Pruning also produces fruitfulness. In the New Testament the figure of good fruit represents the product of a godly life:

> *"Produce fruit in keeping with repentance"* (Matthew 3:8).

Repentance is not merely a change of mind as we see so often with many marginal Christians today, but a radical change in one's life as a whole which involves forsaking sin, and fully turning around to a fruitful life in agreement with God through:

- Cleansing (see vv. 2, 3)
- Abiding (see John 13:10)
- Obedience (see vv. 10, 12)

It is imperative that we restore such teaching and practice of truth in our local churches, that we may have true faith for the final hour.

STUDY SUMMARY: CHAPTER 6

1. The Holy Spirit came with a three-fold mission:
    1.
    2.
    3.

2. We must _____ and _____ truth in order to know it.
3. Sanctification means constant _____.
4. True discipleship consists of first _____ and then _____ the Lord.
5. True disciples move by faith not necessarily _____ to the intellect.
6. The Holy Spirit is the _____ of _____ in Christ.
7. It is the Spirit's work to _____ _____ and to perfect the new life within.
8. The Holy Spirit works in tandem with the _____ of _____.
9. We are cleansed by God's gracious justification, _____ _____.
10. We need sanctification which is _____ _____.
11. Most people know – but few have ever experienced _____ _____.
12. Jesus said, "If you abide in My Word, you shall _____ the _____.
13. The disciple yields to the leading of the Holy Spirit on the strength of the Lord's many _____ and His _____ faithfulness.
14. We receive both justification and sanctification in the new birth. True or False?
15. To receive the full blessedness of knowing Christ the disciple must:
    1. _____ to Christ
    2. _____ to His Word
    3. _____ what appears impossible.

STEWARD LEADERSHIP

CHAPTER 7

CHRIST IS HEAD – THE ULTIMATE REALITY

"God placed all things under his feet, and appointed him to be head over everything, which is his body, the fullness of him who fills everything in every way" (Ephesians 1:22, 23).

I n the great Book of Ephesians, which many theologians consider to be the manual for the church, we find a prayer wherein Paul pleads:

- That the God of our Lord Jesus Christ, the Father of glory, may give you the Spirit of wisdom and revelation in the knowledge of Him (see v. 17).
- That the eyes of your understanding be enlightened (see v. 18a).
- That we might grasp the hope set before us in the resurrected Christ (see v. 18b).
- That we might know what are the riches of the glory of His inheritance in the saints (see v. 18c).

- That in the resurrected Jesus, you and I have the promised unleashed power now (see v. 19).
- That Jesus is God's gift to us, appointed to be head over everything for us (see vv. 20-21).

The great resurrection power unleashed to the saints infuses the church today; that is to those churches that honor and commit to the Headship of Christ!

Biblical Headship

It is imperative that we understand the role Jesus plays in the church today and; thereby insure that we do not overstep our function as human leaders in Christ's body [a metaphor of God's redeemed people, used exclusively in the New Testament of the church]. Thus, it is vitally important that we thoroughly understand what it means for anyone to be "head!"

Old Testament

In the Old Testament the term head [*r'osh*] was applied to human leaders. Their headship included an authority that was judicial and/or authoritative. Also leadership was organized into hierarchies. Institutions were set up by procedures as in the case of Moses, who followed the advice of Jethro to "select capable men from among the people – men who fear God, trustworthy men who hate dishonest gain. Appoint them as officials over thousands, hundreds, fifties, and tens" (see Exodus 18:21). Moses delegated authority – and he only took the most difficult cases.

Moses' hierarchical or top-down concept of "headship" remains the most familiar and popular concept of headship to this day. There is no other way for such secular institutions as the military, corporations, governments at all levels and sad to say, many institutional churches. This headship concept negates the concept of true biblical headship.

New Testament

The New Testament uses the Greek word translated "head," *(kephale)* and it is not the same. In *A Theology of Church Leadership*, Lawrence

O. Richards and Clyde Hoeldtke make a number of observations that are very important when considering the New Testament concept as compared to the Old Testament concept. Careful study of this topic will answer many questions concerning the failure of our churches today.

In their research the authors found that in the gospels, thirty one of the thirty three usages speak of a person's head. The other two refer to the *"head of the corner"* (i.e. cornerstone). In Acts, one of the five occurrences also refers to the cornerstone; the other four refer to someone's physical head. There are twelve occurrences in the Epistles, most referring to Jesus as head over the church.[11]

The hierarchical "headship" pattern of leadership, demonstrated so clearly in the institutions of Old Testament Israel, does not find expression in the New Testament.

Neither in any of these nor in Revelation's eighteen uses of "head" is there any indication that "headship" refers to leaders in the body of Christ![12]

Head of the body

The primary reason for this difference between the Testaments is the fact that Jesus is the head of the body (see Ephesians 1:22; 4:15-16; Colossians 1:18). Jesus' church is not an institution – it is an organism which was not seen even in Old Testament prophecy. A living organism can have only one head, and the head can never be "delegated" to other members of the body. The head is in immediate and personal touch with all members. In fact, one member cannot communicate to another except through the head. [i.e. the right hand cannot ask the left hand to help it lift a box] only the head can communicate that command to the left hand].

An institution has no organic relationship between its individual members and its head – therefore, the head must delegate authority and responsibility to others [subordinates]. The distinctions between the two concepts of "headship" are crucial and must be adhered to in our being obedient to our Lord's will and biblical instructions.

We are the body of Christ and Jesus is our Head; therefore organizational structures and leadership functions must vary significantly from those of any other kind of organizations or concepts. To grasp the reality on which our understanding of New Testament church leadership functions must be based; we must accept the necessity in drawing principles and practices from the New Testament.

Many conflicts in the body of Christ today result from these two distinctly different concepts of church leadership striving to survive in the local church or auxiliary. For those churches that follow principles of leadership from the Old Testament or other hierarchal concepts wherein the members associate with one another in the institutional top-down delegation of authority – Jesus as the Head is denied and replaced by a person. Thus many of the New Testament principles dealing with headship are overshadowed or ignored in separate publications or disciplines produced by the hierarchy. The main qualification of the men selected in Acts 6 was that they be filled with the Holy Spirit; which means they were to be Spirit-led [oneness]. This has to be mandatory and thoroughly understood in the church otherwise you will find yourself involved with Old Testament concepts of law which denies the Holy Spirit and grace. Paul had much to say in condemnation of a concept that tries to mix law and grace. The institutional concept often relies heavily upon natural abilities, and secular preparation. Those of us who exercised hierarchal concept of leadership in the military, police or other disciplined profession prior to entering pastoral ministry must be retrained and redirected by the Holy Spirit. Ministers who come from such careers as will have a hard time adjusting from law to grace wherein the heart knowledge rather than head knowledge is the way. Without proper teaching and training these leaders will lean to secular styles, traditions, customs, written standards, constitutions and by-laws many of which in actuality replace many New Testament truths and principles.

Then there is the "touch not God's anointed" concept wherein the leadership is believed to be more holy and more spiritual then the others, so they project themselves as "above" their people. The head table for these people is always present. God forbid! Christ's style of leadership which we are to follow places us "among" not "above."

Body leadership requires concepts and methodology that is the direct opposite of what was learned and practiced in the secular world. Oneness or unity is the key to the church as an organism [One Lord, One faith, and One baptism]. Emphasis added.

True and false wisdom

In many churches using the hierarchal concept today, earthly wisdom trumps the wisdom of God. What is the difference? In the third chapter of the Book of James, the writer contrasts the two:

Earthly wisdom (false)

• The wisdom that descends not from above is earthly, sensual, and devilish (v. 15). Anything that emanates from hell is certain to have evil results. James spoke to those who would teach. It is easy to claim wisdom, but such self-proclaimed wisdom is seldom true wisdom. False wisdom manifests itself in "bitter envy and strife" (KJV). He has more to say about this selfish ambition, jealousy, envy and strife in verse 16. However, the point is clear, where these qualities are found there is absolutely no reason to boast about any supposed wisdom. Such boasting would be a lie against the truth because the character of life obviously is contrary to true wisdom.

   Because of its source, false wisdom is a dangerous and deadly thing. Since, "this wisdom does not come from above – it is earthly, unspiritual, and demonic." It's important to remember that wisdom cannot be equated with intelligence or knowledge. One may have great intelligence and still have little or no wisdom. One may have acquired great knowledge and a fine education, but this is no guarantee that he or she has wisdom.

   It is sad to say that both great knowledge and fine education has given the perception that this is all that's necessary for a great church, and certainly we have seen enough of such churches. Christ and the Holy Spirit are easily overshadowed in these churches. Tradition and no change are their watchwords. What a hindrance! However, these same qualities intelligence and education under the full control of the Holy Spirit with wisdom from above [more later] puts a "sweet hum" in the ministries of the church and delights any pastor [words like love, joy, and peace are mainstays]. This church lives to the glory of God!

James spoke of false wisdom as earthly which signifies that it is concerned with earthly things rather than with man's relationship with God. In His conversation with Nicodemus, Jesus spoke of earthly things as being distinct from heavenly things such as the new birth (see John 3:3, 16). He also wrote of earthly bodies in contrast to heavenly bodies (1 Corinthians 15:40). The usage closet to that of James's is Philippians 3:19, where Paul wrote of those who mind earthly things.

The term "earthly" is sometimes translated "sensual" (KJV) or "unspiritual" (RSV). The term refers to the natural person as he or she is considered separate and apart from the working of the Holy Spirit. The closest usage is 1 Corinthians 2:14. Paul asserts that,

"A natural man does not receive the things of the Spirit of God, for they are foolishness to him [or her]; and he is not able to know them because they are spiritually discerned."

Thus, the unspiritual or sensual man or woman is the natural person. He or she is without benefit of God's redemption and mercy. False wisdom is wreaking havoc across the church spectrum in America as the secular worldview strives to uproot the biblical worldview even in the church. False wisdom has its ultimate source in Satan and is communicated to people by his servants. All of our institutions to include many local churches are infested with these individuals. Instead of working for the good of the possessor, false wisdom actually works against him or her. Instead of helping the churches, it harms them. God is not pleased and neither should we be!

Heavenly wisdom (true)

- If anything is real, it must show itself in the way the individual lives. This can be said of false wisdom, and it is equally true of the wisdom which is from above. True wisdom comes only as a gift from God (1:5).

The wisdom that is from above is first pure, then peaceable, gentle, and easily entreated, full of mercy and good fruits, without partiality and hypocrisy (v. 17).

True wisdom shows itself in purity of life. It avoids not only the gross sins but all sins. Purity of life is an essential quality for the man or woman of God. Jesus said, "Blessed are the pure in heart, for they shall see God" (Matthew 5:8).

True wisdom leads one to be peaceable. Again, the Beatitude is recalled: "Blessed are the peacemakers, for they shall be called sons of God" (Matthew 5:9). This is the opposite of the bitter jealousy and selfish ambition which James said were the characteristics of false wisdom. A sign of wisdom is being anxious to live at peace with fellowman. This is a sign of wisdom.

True wisdom leads to gentleness in life. It carries the idea of that which is fitting or fair and equitable. Wisdom does not deal harshly with others.

True wisdom is compliant. This means he or she is "easy to entreat" (KJV), and teachable. This person is not closed-minded. He or she can be approached and expected to listen to all sides before making up his or her mind.

True wisdom leads to mercy and good fruits. In James 2:13 the writer referred to the place of mercy in the life of the believer: "For judgment is without mercy to him [or her] that does not show mercy." The individual who does not show consideration, love and kindness in any way does not have the wisdom that come from God above.

True wisdom is without partiality and without hypocrisy. This person has no room for uncertainty or indecision, but is sincere. Wisdom gives a fair and honest picture at all times.

The welcomed distortion

More often than not the concept we have of "headship" in the churches reflects the Old Testament hierarchical leadership structure, I call it the Moses model. This distortion seen in contemporary churches is actually an adaptation of the secular concept and model; which as I said earlier stops or hinders the Holy Spirit's supernatural work.

The top-down organizations in many traditional churches have been around for generations and many see no need for change – especially where power, money and authority are challenged. "We have always done it that way!" Often this saying has been referred to as the "seven last words of a dying church!" These individuals have to rely on earthly wisdom.

Sometime ago I had a conversation with a pastor of a well-known institutional church. We began to talk about needed restoration in the church toward ministry. He pulled out one of his church bulletins and proudly showed me that he had changed all the titles of the church's auxiliaries and boards to ministries [i.e. deacons' ministry, ushers' ministry, and music ministry]. Name changing was the extent of his renovation. God forbid!

My first response is we do not live in ordinary times. Changes in our society are more radical and rapid today than they have ever been; and demanding changes in the church. Just think how we've gone from the old bulky G-1 bag car phones of the 90's to the sleek G-4's of today, I-phones, smart phones and TV's, computers and much more.

If not careful those proverbial people who always suggest that we wait awhile or take it slow every time innovation is proposed – the new thing may well pass us by having effected society in general and our churches in particular.

This applies especially to the institutional churches. Sixty or so years ago churches seemed to operate on an unspoken assumption that denominational churches would be the same yesterday, today, and forever.

Today things are definitely not as they were. Many new churches are springing up that would be almost unrecognizable to the generations of believers that have passed on before us. Additionally, few parents today who belong to denominational churches are surprised or bothered when their young people decide to join other, more contemporary churches.

Even inside traditional churches, many things – from dress codes, to styles of worship are much different than they were twenty years ago. For whatever reason, many churches do not make sure before baptism that their candidates have experienced clear and authentic conversion. Others accept people into membership with no assurance they have been "born again" as a biblical prerequisite (see John 3:3).

Many people are seeking a spiritual experience and sadly there are many counterfeits available to the culture and wider society introduced through multiculturalism [with its many gods] subtly embedded in our educational system at all levels – at the exclusion of the God of the Bible and His Son, Jesus Christ. However, they can have the authentic experience; which is in Christ Jesus if we tell them about Him! Radical reformation is now a reality of life in those churches listening to the Holy Spirit.

Take your ministry to the world

When Jesus walked the earth 2000 years ago, He touched the problems of society through one physical body – His own! Today in the 21st century, He carries on the same work through a corporate body that exists around the world, imbedded in every level and area of society. It is His spiritual creation, the church, the body of Christ.

The ministry committed to the body of Christ [the church] is to the same humanity that Jesus ministered to, experiencing the same issues, problems, attitudes, and conditions. The same Holy Spirit who guided Christ empowers and guides us through love and Spiritual gifts which He gives believers severely as He wills (see 1 Corinthians 12:11).

Only when a Christian uses his or her spiritual gifts in the power of the Holy Spirit is their life representative of Christ in the world. We must remember the two-fold reason for the giving of spiritual gifts:

1) To do the work of ministry – evangelize the world, and
2) To building up the body of Christ – edifying the church

It is clearly the Lord's desire that, Christ be manifested to the world through the work of His true church. However, He never intended for the world to have to come to the church to find Christ! Instead, He intended that the church move out into the world. God designed the church to be present in the world and visible in the marketplaces and public squares around the world.

When the world is able to see the Spirit-filled body of Christ among them, challenging, loving and reaching them, they will understand that Jesus Christ is very much alive. And His life is being reproduced in ordinary believers by the Holy Spirit!

The fruit of the new man

> *"Let the word of Christ dwell in you richly in all wisdom; teaching and admonishing one another in psalms and hymns, and spiritual songs, singing with grace in your hearts to the Lord. And whatever you do in word or deed, do all in the name of the Lord Jesus, giving thanks to God the Father through Him"* (Colossians 316-17).

> *"But above all these things put on love, which is the bond of perfection"* (v. 14).

Jesus is Lord! Jesus is Lord of all or Lord of none. The new spiritual creation that Christ is building today is exact, in other words He requires our very lives. We are to give ourselves away for the sake of others. In the verses above the Apostle Paul gave us a word picture of what we'll look like.

> *"Do not lie to one another, since you have put off the old man with his deeds, and have put on the new man who is renewed in knowledge according to the image of Him who created him"* (Colossians 3:10). Emphasis added.

Paul began with "do not lie to one another." Much of the vernacular used in welcoming new converts into the local church does not mention Christ. Some people are deceived to believe that it's okay to simply welcome the unsaved into church membership. Neither is the kingdom of God mentioned.

In his discourses, Paul makes clear that accepting Christ as our personal Savior is the beginning of the salvation process. Jesus said, "You must be born again" (John 3:3). Then He went to the cross to complete the way back to the Father for us. So you can hear the gospel of Christ:

Justification

Hear the gospel receive it and experience radical repentance, which means changing our thinking and agreeing with God that I am a sinner. When I receive His forgiveness the divine exchange takes place as God was in Christ reconciling the world wherein He made possible a way to change the sinner's status bringing him or her from alienation to a state of forgiveness and right relationship with God (Corinthians 5:18-20).

"For God so loved the world that H gave His only begotten Son, that whoever believes in Him should not perish but have everlasting life" (John 3:16).

"For He made Him who knew no sin to be sin for us, that we might become the righteousness of God in Him" (2 Corinthians 5:21).

The Father gave His unique and beloved Son to die on behalf of sinful men. He took my sins and gave me His righteousness – the divine exchange. Here is summarized the doctrine of justification [the cross].

God treated Him as if He committed believers sins – and treats believers as if they did only the righteous deeds of the sinless Son of God.

Sanctification

To our shame, often the new believer is justified and then left to fend for him or herself. The old church use to teach that the new believer is like a new-born baby, a complete human being, but he or she is immature and must be nurtured to full development and become strong and mature. The church must have in place a process that will form new Christians into committed disciples. The process must be clearly rooted in the biblical mandate to make disciples.

Many churches turn the process of formation or sanctification into a program which undermines its very purpose. Sanctification is a spiritual process that the Holy Spirit sets in motion to engage the heart, the mind, the will, indeed the whole man – in a lifelong commitment of discipleship.

Character of the new man

> *Therefore if any is in Christ,*
> *He is a new creature:*
> *Old things are passed away;*
> *Behold,*
> *All things are become new.*

Again, in conversion the believer is spiritually reborn and a new-born babe in Christ with a capacity to grow and mature in spirit. Spiritual growth in Christ as a maturing disciple produces fruit. We can't keep letting the devil move the stakes on our receiving the character of Christ. One day if you are not careful, he'll move it to a position just on the other side of the grave and your next step will be short and you will land in the grave with your work undone. We are told in verse 8 to put off these:

- Anger
- Wrath
- Malice
- Blasphemy
- Filthy language
- Do not lie to one another

Since you have put off the old man [the old unregenerate self which originated in Adam (see Romans 5:12-14; 6:6; and Ephesians 4:22). It's like one pulling off a dirty shirt. Because the old man died in Christ and the new man lives in Christ – this is a fact of new spiritual creation:

> *"And all things are of God, who has reconciled us to Himself by Christ Jesus, and has given unto us the ministry of reconciliation"* (2 Corinthians 5:18).

The believer's new spiritual perception of everything is a constant reality for him or her now living for eternity not temporal things. Sinners on their own cannot participate in these new realities. James identifies this transformation as the faith that produces works (see James 2:14-25; Ephesians 2:10). The new spiritual life provides:

- Radical repentance
- Personal holiness
- New divinely given life
- New quality of life (which never existed before)

You must have a deep through *knowledge* of the will of God as revealed in the Word of God. The Word of God transforms you by renewing your mind/ changes your thinking. Therefore the disciples are to "put on:"

- Tender mercies
- Kindness
- Humility
- Meekness
- Longsuffering
- Bearing with one another
- Forgiving one another; even as Christ forgave you

But above all these things put on love, which is the bond of perfection.

Serving the Lord

In their book *Experiencing God,* Henry T. Blackaby and Claude V. King summed up reality this way, "What our world often sees are devoted, committed Christians serving God. But they are not seeing God. They comment, "Well, there's a wonderful, dedicated, committed group of people serving God." They, however, do not see anything happening that can *only be explained in terms of the activity of God.* Why? Simply, because we are not attempting anything that only God can do."

Further, "Our world is not attracted to the Christ we serve because they cannot see Him at work. They do not hesitate to attack the Christian position on morality because they have no fear of the God we serve. The world is passing us by because they do not want to get involved in what they see. They are not having an opportunity to see God. Let the world see God at work, and He will attract people to Himself. Let Christ be lifted up – not in words, but in life.[13]

Let them see the difference that a living Christ makes in a life, a family, or a church; that will make a difference in how they respond. When the world see things happening through God's people that cannot be explained except that God Himself has done them, then the world will be drawn to the God they see. Let world leaders see the miraculous signs of an all-powerful God, and they, like Nebuchadnerzzar, will declare that He is the one true God.

STUDY SUMMARY: CHAPTER 7

1. The resurrection power is _____ to those churches that honor and commit to the _____ of Christ.
2. Moses' top down concept of _____ remains the most popular secular concept of _____ to this day.
3. _____ _____ is a metaphor of God's redeemed children.
4. The old hierarchical pattern of leadership of the Old Testament does not find _____ in the New Testament.
5. Describe the distinction between the two concepts of leadership discussed in this chapter in the space below:
6. Jesus' church is not an institution, it is an _____.
7. An institution has no organic relationship between individual members and the head; therefore the head must _____ authority and responsibility.
8. In order to understand leadership functions, we must draw _____ and _____ from the New Testament.
9. Jesus Christ and the Holy Spirit are denied in many churches that follow the _____ _____ concept.
10. The Holy Spirit _____ and _____ us through spiritual gifts which He gives severely as He wills.
11. Christians are _____ representatives in the world.
12. Christ's life is being reproduced in others by the _____ _____.

13. After reading chapter 7, what was said about the loss of members in the local church?
14. People are drawn to God when things are happening in the church that can only be attributed to _____.
15. What must happen before world leaders see God?

CHAPTER 8

THE BODY OF CHRIST – THE CHURCH

"For as the body is one and has many members,
But all the members of that one body,
being many, are one body,
so also is Christ"
(1 Corinthians 12:12).

We do not truly realize the power that is available to us. Jesus intended for His church to exert great power ["dunamus"][14] in this dark and dangerous world. Look again at Acts 1:8, "You shall receive power *[dunamus]* after the Holy Spirit has come upon you ...." In reality, the church is the most powerful force on earth. Perhaps you are asking, "What keeps us from experiencing that power now?" The major problem we face is failure to read, follow instructions, disobedience, and unbelief! This condition is the result of spiritual ignorance on a major scale. Most Christians tragically have no idea, what the biblical pattern really is for the church.

Whenever the church follows the biblical Holy Spirit powered [dunamus] pattern designed by God and described by the Bible – it becomes the most amazing, dynamic, and powerful world-changing force on earth.

We find God's truth and directions about His church throughout the New Testament, and especially in the Apostle Paul's writings. His letters written specifically to Timothy and Titus and specifically his own letter to the Ephesians deal with the function of the church, and its essential relationship to the Lord, and like so much of his other writing, underscore the truth that:

- Salvation is by faith alone; and not through works or human efforts.
- The first half of the epistle (chapters 1-3) addresses the central doctrines of the Christian faith.
- The second half of the letter (chapters 4-6) describes how those spiritual truths are to be reflected in the Christian's character and then in spiritual conflict with the forces of evil.[15]

The whole letter emphasizes the truth that all believers are united in Christ because the church is the one body of Christ. Paul describes how God formed this new spiritual creation from Jews and Gentiles with His Son as the Head.

The Work of Ministry

The Lord has endowed His corporate body with a number of spiritual gifts designed to build-up [edify] in a growing manner so that each individual can maintain a right relationship with God. These gifts are to be used in the power of the Holy Spirit in ministry to the world as a result of Christ's life within. One term Paul used to describe the spiritual gifts is *service*. Seen from this perspective the gifts are a service for the church and the wider community.

Spiritual gifts are not for the Christian's personal use to be worn as a badge of courage or pride – but are used through the Christians by the Spirit. Paul notes concerning Christ's new spiritual creation:

> *"There is neither Jew nor Greek, there is neither slave nor free, there is neither male nor female: for you are all one in Christ Jesus. And if you are Christ's, then you are Abraham's seed, and heirs according to the promise"* (Galatians 3:28-29).

Rather than concerning ourselves with gender, one of the gravest hindrances to the work of effective ministry concerns two philosophies of ministry; which all Christians should be familiar within America's local churches:

- First – there are those who hold that truth is attained through science and reason – and they undoubtedly attempt to live by the mixing of law and grace (study carefully Galatians 1:6-10).
- Second – is the fact that truth can only be attained through revelation from God. We walk by faith not by sight; led and gifted of the Spirit. And then after we hear what He is saying to us individually and corporately; take proper action upon His will not ours or any other person's.

Spiritual gifts are resident in the Holy Spirit and when believers are available in word and deed – they can be greatly used of God (see 1 Corinthians 12 and Romans 12). Thus, God has given each one of us a wonderful opportunity to join with Him in His work using the gifts He has entrusted to us.

The reward of finding and putting into practice your spiritual gift or gifts is the personal blessing of knowing that you are biblically in the will of God (study carefully Romans 12:1-6).

The apostle Peter writes, *"As each has received a gift, employ it for one another, as good stewards of God's varied grace"* (1 Peter 4:10). Again, a spiritual gift is a specific capacity or function given to each true Christian directly by the Spirit of God.

- What is your spiritual gift?
- Are you operating in your spiritual gift?

It is imperative that we understand that these gifts are not hereditary nor do we generate them ourselves; they are imparted to us by the Holy Spirit Himself. Please note the gifts listed below are in alphabetical order only:

ADMINISTRATION (1 CORINTHIANS 12:28)

This gift is the special anointing that the Spirit gives to certain members of the body of Christ to understand clearly the immediate and long range goals of a particular unit of the body of Christ and to devise and execute plans for the accomplishment of those goals (see Acts 27:11).

APOSTLE (Ephesians 4:11)

This gift is the special anointing that God gives to certain members of the body of Christ to assume and exercise general leadership over a number of churches or ministries (that they have established) with extraordinary authority in spiritual matters which are spontaneously recognized by these churches. For an example (see 1 Thessalonians 2:6).

CELIBACY (1 Corinthians 7:7-8)

This is the special anointing that God gives to certain members of the body of Christ to remain single and enjoy it; to be unmarried and not suffer undue sexual temptations. For examples (see Matthew 19:10-12 "for Christ's sake").

DISCERNING OF SPIRITS (1 Corinthians 12:10)

This gift is the special anointing that the Spirit gives to certain members of the body of Christ [all mature Christians should have this gift] to know with assurance whether certain behavior purported to be of God is really divine, human, or satanic. For example (see 1 Thessalonians 6:1-6).

EVANGELIST (Ephesians 4:11)

This gift is the special anointing that the Spirit gives to certain members of the body of Christ to share the Gospel with unbelievers in such a way that men and women become Jesus' disciples and responsible members of the body of Christ. For examples (see Acts 8:4-6; 21:8; 8:26-40).

EXHORTATION (Romans 12:6-8)

This gift is the special anointing to minister words of comfort, consolation, encouragement, and counsel to other members of the body of Christ in such a way that they feel helped and healed. For example (see 2 Corinthians 1:1-7 "God of all comfort").

EXORCISM (Acts 8:1-4)

This gift is the special anointing to cast out demons and evil spirits. For example (see Acts 16:16-18 "Paul and the slave girl").

FAITH (Ephesians 2:8)

This gift is the special anointing to discern with extraordinary confidence the will and purpose of God for the future of His work. [For all Christians] For example (see Matthew 17:14-21 "move mountains").

GIVING (Romans 12:8)

This gift is the special anointing to contribute material resources to the work of the Lord with liberality and cheerfulness (see Philippians 4:16-19).

HEALING (1 Corinthians 12:9, 28, 30)

This gift is the special anointing to serve as human intermediaries through whom it pleases God to cure illness and restore health apart from the use of natural means. For example (see Matthew 8:1-4 "the leper).

<u>HELPS </u>(1 Corinthians 12:28)

This gift is the special anointing to invest the talents one has in the life and ministry of others of the body, thus enabling the person to increase the effectiveness of his or her spiritual gifts. For example (see Acts 9:36).

<u>HOSPITALITY</u> (1 Peter 4:9-10)

This is a special anointing to provide an open house and a warm welcome for those in need of food and lodging. For example (see Hebrews 13:1-2 "strangers").

<u>INTERCESSION </u>(Romans 8:26-27)

This gift is the special anointing to pray for extended periods of time on a regular basis and see frequent and specific answers to their prayers to a degree such greater than the average Christian. For example (see Colossians 4:12 "Epaphras").

"Much prayer – much power and little prayer – little power"

<u>INTERPRETATION OF TONGUES</u> (1 Corinthians 12:10)

This gift is the special anointing given to certain members of the body of Christ to make known in the vernacular the message of one who speaks in tongues.

<u>KNOWLEDGE</u> (1 Corinthians 12:8)

This gift is a special anointing to discover, analyze, and clearly clarify ideas which are pertinent to the growth and well being of the church. For example (see 1 Corinthians 8:1-2 "without pride").

LEADERSHIP (Romans 12:8)

This gift is the special anointing to set goals in accordance with God's purpose for the future and to communicate these goals to others in such a way that they voluntarily and harmoniously work together to accomplish those goals for the glory of God. For example (see 1 Timothy 3-5 "family" "church").

MARTYDOM (1 Corinthians 13:1-3, 8)

This gift is the special anointing to undergo suffering for the faith even to the point of death while consistently displaying a joyous and victorious attitude which brings glory to God. For example (see Acts 20:24 "Death is ok").

MERCY (Romans 12:8)

This gift is the special anointing to feel genuine empathy and compassion for individuals, both Christian and non-Christian, who suffer distressing physical, mental, or emotional problems and to translate that compassion into fully-done deeds which reflect Christ's love and alleviate suffering. For example (see Luke 17:11-14 "debilitating disease").

MIRACLES (1 Corinthians 12:10, 28)

This gift is the special anointing to serve as intermediaries through whom it pleases God to perform powerful acts that are perceived by observers to have altered the ordinary course of nature For example (see Acts 9:36-41 "Tabitha").

MISSIONARY (1 CORINTHIANS 9:19-23)

This gift is the special anointing to minister whatever other spiritual gifts they have in a second culture. For example (see Galatians 2:7-14 "Paul").

PASTOR (Ephesians 4:11)

This gift is the special anointing to assume a personal responsibility for the spiritual warfare of a group of believers. For example (see Hebrews 13:7, 17 "leads").

PROPHET (Ephesians 4:11)

This gift is the special anointing to receive and communicate an immediate message of God to His people through a divinely-appointed utterance. For example (see Acts 21:10, 11 "Agabus").

SERVICE (Romans 12:6, 7)

This gift is a special anointing to identify the unmet needs involved in a task related to God's work, and to make use of available resources to meet those needs and help accomplish the desired goals. For example (see Luke 22:24-27 "others").

TEACHER (Ephesians 4:11)

This gift is a special anointing to communicate information relevant to the health and ministry of the body of Christ and its members in such a way that others will learn. For example (see Ephesians 4:13-14 "not wavering").

TONGUES (1 Corinthians 12:10, 28)

This gift is the special anointing to speak to God in a language they have never learned and to receive and communicate an immediate message of God to His people through divinely anointed utterance. For example (see Acts 10:24-28 (Gentiles").

VOLUNTARY POVERTY (1 Corinthians 13:1-3)

This gift is a special anointing to renounce material comfort and luxury and adopt a personal lifestyle equivalent to those living at the poverty level in a given society in order to serve God more effectively. For example (see Matthew 8:20 "Jesus").

WISDOM (1 Corinthians 12:7, 8)

This gift is the special anointing to know the mind of the Christ in such a way as to receive insight into how given knowledge may best be applied to specific needs arising in the body of Christ. For example (see James 1:5-6 "ask").[16]

Remember, the ultimate purpose of spiritual gifts is for the edification and unity of the body of Christ. The Holy Spirit accomplishes this by enabling individual members of the body to be effective in radical restoration and renewal, "Till we all come into the unity of the faith, and of the knowledge of the fullness of Christ: that we henceforth be no more children, tossed to and fro, and carried about with every wind and doctrine, by the sleight of men, and cunning craftiness, whereby they lie in wait to receive" (Ephesians 4:13-14).

STUDY GUIDE: CHAPTER 8

1. The church is the most _____ _____ on earth.
2. Most Christians do not know what the _____ pattern is for the church.
3. The first half of the Book of Ephesians (chapters 1-3) addresses the _____ _____ of the faith.
4. The second half (chapters 4-6) describes the spiritual truths to be reflected in the Christian's _____ and then in _____ conflict with the forces of evil.
5. This chapter discussed two philosophies of ministries practiced in the American church. Explain each below:
   a.
   b.

6. Truth can only be attained through _____ from God.
7. We walk by _____ not by _____.
8. We hear the Spirit; and then take proper _____.
9. What is your spiritual gift (s)?
10. Are you operating in your spiritual gift (s)?
11. It is imperative that we understand That spiritual gifts are not _____ nor do we _____ them.
12. One term the apostle Paul used to describe the spiritual gifts is _____.
13. What does Galatians 3:28-29 say about Christ's new creation?
    a.

14. Spiritual truths are to be reflected in the Christian's _____.
15. What is the ultimate goal and purpose of spiritual gifts?
    a.

THE GOAL OF EQUIPPING THE SAINTS

Throughout the Reformation and even until today, no concept of church ministry has proved more radical and bitterly fought – than Ephesians 4 that places the work of the church squarely into the hands of the saints, ordinary Christian men, women, girls and boys; not to be done by professional clergy or a few selected laypersons. Notice again Paul's message that the five offices of: apostles, prophets, evangelists, pastors, and teachers exist solely to insure that the saints move through three stages of growth: 1) the equipping of the saints; 2) for the work of ministry; 3) for edifying or building up the body of Christ; all with the final goal of maturity, truth, love and unity (Ephesians 4:12). Please note neither of the ministers listed above are expected to do the work of ministry!

Light bearers

"Therefore be imitators of God as dear children. And walk in love, as Christ also has loved us and given Himself for us, an offering and a sacrifice to God for a sweet-smelling aroma" (Ephesians 5:1-3).

How well do I remember our three girls and two boys, our little children, all grown now with their own families? Those two sons would go where I went if they were allowed to – they followed in my footsteps.

I recall a story I heard some time ago about a drunkard who was on his way to the bar to get a drink early one morning after a beautiful snow had fallen the night before. As he walked through the snow, his feet left imprints. He had a little boy about five years old .... Which he love very dearly. He loved the boy more than he loved his own life. He had not gone far when he heard a crouching noise in the snow behind him.

He turned to look back, it was his little son. The boy was stretching his little legs trying to step into each of his father's footprints. The father said, "Son what are you doing?" The boy replied, "Daddy, I am following in your footprints." The story goes that instead of to the bar, the father picked up the little boy in his arms, pulled him close, wrapped his coat around the shivering little body and returned home, never to enter a bar again. Why? He was setting a life pattern for his son to follow. Today many people come to the same crossroad with their children, but through self-centeredness continue on to the bar [many times destroying both lives]. We are to be Christ-centered, then as children of God, [His light bearers], we should walk in His steps before our children and others:

- We are not to walk in Jesus' footsteps because we are afraid not to.
- We are not to give up bad habits and behavior because the church doctrine declares that we should not go certain places and do certain things.

If you give up a filthy habit because that is the rule in your church, then God gets no glory, and you get no eternal profit for giving it up; but if you give up the lust of the flesh and the habits of the world because you love Jesus, and stay away from things that does not bring glory to God because you love Jesus, then you will be blessed, the body of Christ will be blessed, and heaven will be blessed because of your sacrificial living in love.

True born again children of God are:

1. *Children of love* – because our Spiritual Father is love. He who does not love does not know God, for God is love (1 John 4:8).
2. *Children of light* – Our heavenly Father is light. "In Him was life, and the life was the light of men. And the light shines in the darkness, and the darkness did not comprehend it" (John 1:4-5). "But you, brethren, are not in darkness, so that this Day should overtake you as a thief. You are all sons of light and sons of the day. We are not of the night or of darkness. Therefore let us not sleep, as others do, but let us watch and be sober. For those who sleep at night and those who get drunk are drunk at night" (1 Thessalonians 5:4-7).

As the moon has no light of its own, but reflects the light of the sun – so may we be reminded as children of light, we have no light of our own, but we are to reflect the light of the Son!

---

3. *Children of wisdom* – Our God and our Christ are wisdom. *"The fear of the Lord is the beginning of knowledge: but fools despise wisdom and instruction"* (Proverbs 1:7). No flesh should glory in His presence. But of Him you are in Christ Jesus, who became for us wisdom from God – and righteousness and sanctification and redemption – that, as it is written, *"He who glories, let him glory in the LORD"* (1 Corinthians 1:29-31).

The essence of Christianity

If God treated humankind like some Christians treat each other – and like some Christians treat their unsaved neighbors and friends, this earth would be a place of untold agony. Jesus loved His enemies:

- He did not compromise with them.
- He did not love their sin.
- But He loved them.

Love is the essence of Christianity and if we do not love our fellow humans whom we see, how can we love God whom we can not see? We love Him, because He first loved us – and if we are born again, and spiritually-minded as we should be, we will display love in all of our daily dealings in life.

Take counsel from the apostle Paul, who lists the spiritual gifts that the Holy Spirit gives to us in 1 Corinthians 12. Then he gives us the operation [the how to] of the gifts in chapter 14. However, to get from the giving of the gift to the operation and practice of the gift – we must go through chapter 13 [agape love]. Put plainly, he said,

1. Now concerning spiritual gifts brethren, I do not want you to be ignorant (see 1 Corinthians 12:1).
2. Pursue love and desire spiritual gifts (see 1 Corinthians 14:1).
3. Though I have the gift of prophecy [or any other gift], and understand all mysteries and all knowledge, and though I have all faith, so that I could remove mountains, but have not love, *I am nothing* (see 1 Corinthians 13:2).

Love never fails

This uncompromising and bold affirmation introduces the contrast of love with the spiritual gifts which will not last. Paul wants the Corinthian Christians [and us] to know that all gifts, especially tongues, which attracted [and attracts today] their attention so much would one day no longer be needed. But love would continue forever. We are warned here not to allow our gifts to outrun our character. Love is the first fruit of the Spirit (see Galatians 5:22).

In order to walk in victory over the lust of the flesh we are to live step-by-step in the power of the Holy Spirit as He works through *our spirit. If we live in the Spirit, let us also walk in the Spirit* (v. 25). Walking each moment by faith in God's Word under the control of the Holy Spirit assures us of absolute victory over the desires or works of the flesh.

In Ephesians 5:18 we are admonished: *"And do not be drunk with wine, in which is dissipation; but be filled with the Spirit"* Just as a person who is drunk with wine is under the control of alcohol – so a Spirit-filled Christian is controlled by the Spirit. The tense of the Greek word translated *filled* indicates that filling is a moment-by-moment, repeatable action. [Emphasis added].

The work of the church for which we, [the five ministers of Ephesians 4:11] are equipping the saints to pursue is a supernatural work – impossible to be accomplished in our own natural strength! One reason so many churches face defeat today is they are continuously following church concepts wherein nothing is ever attempted or done that cannot be accomplished **without** the presence and power of the Holy Spirit.

The goal is unity

"I therefore, the prisoner of the Lord, beseech you to walk worthy of the calling with which you were called, with all lowliness and gentleness, with longsuffering, bearing with one another in love, endeavoring to keep the unity of the Spirit in the bond of peace" (Ephesians 4:1-3).

In the passage above it is clear that we are admonished to walk worthy – for unity. All believers are to work at keeping the peace in order to remain bound together in the unity of the Spirit. Jesus has broken down every wall or partition existing between human beings.

Sad to say, not every believer walks in the Spirit – not all the time. Some believers allow self and the old life to re-enter the picture and up pops their old:

- Prejudices
- Differences
- Hurts
- Jealousies
- Complaints
- Criticisms
- Gripes
- Grumblings
- Pride
- Arrogance
- Comparisons
- Dislikes

Certainly the results are horrific for the church – divisiveness, disturbance of the peace and the spirit of unity. This is the reason for Paul's charge. We normally accept the dictionary definition for the word "endeavor" which means "to try," but conveyed in its usage in this passage means to be diligent, working to take care, doing one's very best, and making haste to do it.[17]

The only way to walk worthy of God's great calling is to work at keeping the peace and unity which God has given us!

Nothing cuts the heart of God like divisiveness between His people. Divisiveness tears His church apart. The church is the very thing God is doing in creating a new spiritual body of people. They will live together in the love and unity of His Son. God expects us to live in the love and unity of His Spirit here and now!

STUDY SUMMARY: CHAPTER 9

1. Ephesians 4 lays the work of the church squarely into the hands of the _____.

2. List the three stages of growth expected of all Christians:
   a.
   b.
   c.

3. As children of God, we are to be Christ-centered and not _____ centered.

4. True born again children of God are:
   - Children of _____.
   - Children of _____.
   - Children of _____.

5. If you give up a bad habit because that is a church rule, then God gets no _____.

6. _____ is the essence of Christianity.

7. As our example, Jesus loved His enemies:
   - He did not _____ with them.
   - He did not _____ their sin.
   - But He _____ them.

8. Paul declares that a spiritual gift without _____ is nothing.

9. Concerning spiritual gifts Paul did not want the people to be _____.

10. To walk in victory we must live step-by-step in the _____ of the Holy Spirit.

11. Equipping cannot take place without the power and _____ of the Holy Spirit.

12. Jesus has broken down every _____ or _____ existing between human beings.

13. Divisiveness among His people cuts the heart of God; as it tears the _____ apart.

14. God expects us to live in the _____ and _____ of the Holy Spirit.

15. Ephesians 5:18 commands, _____ _____ _____ _____ _____.

BODY LEADERSHIP

······················ CHAPTER 10 ·····················

SERVANT-HOOD: A BIBLICAL PERSPECTIVE

"And a servant of the Lord must not quarrel but be gentle to all, able to teach, patient, in humility correcting those who are in opposition, if God perhaps will grant them repentance, so that they may know truth" (2 Timothy 2:24-25).

In our culture "servant-hood" is one of those unmentionables. People strive to be possessors and not the possessed. We are not happy about setting aside our concerns for those of other people. Both servant and slave are equally terms of defamation – words that seem to put down or demean implying a degrading of personal worth and value. It is obvious from these negative connotations that we must develop a biblical perspective. Henry T. Blackaby says, "The call to salvation is a call to be on mission with God. In this new relationship you move into a servant role with God as your Lord and Master."[18]

Other writers define a servant as one who finds out what the master wants done, and then he or she goes off alone and does it. This is not the biblical concept of a servant of God. Being a servant of God is different from being a servant of a human master. A servant of a human master works for his or her master. God however works through His servants. When we come to God as His servant:

- He is like the potter with his clay, He wants to mold and transform you into the instrument of His choice.
- He wants to take your life and put it where He wills.
- He wants to work through you to accomplish His purposes.
- Just as clay cannot do anything on its own, you do not have the ability to do His command anywhere except where the Lord wants you to be.
- In the next section you will see Jesus' example.
- He does His work through you; as you obey.
- You must remain moldable, teachable, and available for the Master's use.

Unlimited Potential

The Master can use any servant He chooses. The servant can do nothing for the kingdom of God by himself or herself. Jesus said, *"The Son of God can do nothing of Himself"* (John 5:19) and *"Without Me you can do nothing"* (John 15:5). When God is working through His servant – that servant has unlimited potential! Servant-hood requires obedience. Who brought water from the rock, Moses or God? God did it! As His servants we must always remember it is God accomplishing the work – not us!

Servant in the Old Testament

Dr. Larry Richards puts forth two primary "servants" in the Old Testament. One is the nation of Israel and the second is the promised Deliverer. The picture of Israel as a servant concerns the purpose for which God chose them. To be named a "servant" by God is definitely not degradation. Notice how special God's servants are to Him. Even when Israel failed in her calling as God's servant, God's commitment to her never faltered – and He has promised to restore her.

The primary Old Testament servant figure is not Israel, but it is the promised Messiah. The Prophet Isaiah prophesied that a Man will come who will be a Servant of the Lord. He will perfectly perform the will of God, and through His obedience win freedom for the captives. Servant-hood in the Old Testament is not a most favored way of life.[19]

In Isaiah 42:1-4 we find a beautiful picture of this Servant, highlighting His relationship to God and His attitude as He goes about His ministry:

> *"Behold! My Servant whom I*
> *uphold,*
> *My Elect One in whom My soul*
> *delights!*
> *I have put My Spirit upon Him,*
> *He will bring forth justice to the*
> *Gentiles.*
> *He will not cry out, nor rise His*
> *voice,*
> *Not cause His voice to be heard in*
> *the street.*
> *A bruised reed He will not break,*
> *And smoking flax He will not*
> *quench;*
> *He will bring forth justice for truth.*
> *He will not fail nor be discouraged,*
> *Till He has established justice in the*
> *earth;*
> *And the coastlands shall wait for His*
> *law."*

The Servant portrayed here, Jesus Christ is a source of special delight for the Lord; and the example to all servants, notice:

- He is gifted with the Spirit.
- He adopts a gentle and quit lifestyle.
- He is for the birth of justice.
- He meets with resistance.
- He is neither discouraged nor fails.
- He succeeds in carrying out the purpose for which He was called.

To Christ and to all godly servants God promises:

> *I the Lord, have called You to righteousness;*
> *I will take hold of Your hand.*
> *I will keep You and will give You*
> *as a covenant to the people......*
> (Isaiah 4:6)

Like our Lord, we have been selected to live and to give ourselves for God's people. Servant-hood is a high and special calling that involves a covenantal relationship with God. There is a willing commitment by the servant to a Master who fully commits Himself to the servant as well.

Leviticus 25 and Exodus 21 give us the controlling Old Testament image of the servant/ master relationship. Leviticus shows a brother Israelite who becomes poor and sells himself to a more prosperous countryman. In that relationship he must never serve as a slave. He is to be treated as a hired worker" (Leviticus 25:40). In the year of Jubilee [the seventh year] he is to be freed to return to his own land or family. But as Exodus points out, such a servant may develop key relationships during his service. So if the servant declares, "I love my master and my wife and my children and do not want to go free," then by the servant's own free choice "he will be his servant for life" (Exodus 21:5-6).

This is the covenantal nature of our relationship to God as servants. He has shaped us and called us to be leaders of His body and committed Himself to be with us always. In return, we commit ourselves to serve Him within the body wherever He chooses to place us.

In the New Testament

Our primary insights into servant-hood in the New Testament are provided in the Gospels in the examples of Jesus. He was the greatest example of servant-hood in the Old Testament – likewise, He is the greatest example of servant-hood in the New Testament. We are called to His lifestyle:

> *"Even the Son of Man did not come to be served, but to serve, and to*
> *give His life as a ransom for many"* (Mark 10:25).

Jesus instructed the twelve and the crowds, as He exposed the false spiritual leadership of the Pharisees. "You have only one Master and you are all brothers." The greatest among you will be your servant. For whoever exalts himself will be humbled, and whoever humbles himself will be exalted" (Matthew 23:8-12).

In private with His disciples, Jesus went beyond talking and used the teachable moment to put His words into a picture they would never forget. In the intimacy of the upper room, Jesus knelt before them and with a towel and basin of water washed their feet. They were embarrassed – it wasn't right that their Lord should stoop before them. But Jesus did. Afterward, He asked them:

> *"Do you understand what I have done for you? You call Me "Teacher" and "Lord," and rightly so, for that is what I am. Now that I, your Lord and Teacher, have washed your feet, you also should wash one another's feet. I have set the example that you should do as I have done for you. I tell you the truth, no servant is greater than his master, nor is a messenger greater than the one who sent him. Once you know these things you will be blessed if you do them"* (John 13:12-17).

Only One Master

It is imperative that all body leaders realize that Jesus Christ, the Head is the only Head of His body; and the church is to trust Him! Today we are constantly bombarded with bad press wherein a servant or servants have violated their covenantal relationship with God by going to secular courts and other agencies of the world trying to resolve church matters that really require spiritual or biblical solutions. While the servant's profile in both the Old and New Testament may appear to denigrate the servant, our covenant relationship with God's promises to take care of us should be sufficient. Do you trust Him? Christ remains our only example in the Old and New Testaments – we had better receive His words and be blessed wherever He assigns us.

STUDY SUMMARY: CHAPTER 10

1. We are not happy about setting aside our _____
    for those of other people.
2. Due to the negative connotations concerning the words
    _____ and _____, we must develop a biblical
    perspective.
3. To be named a "servant" by God definitely is
    not _____.
4. The primary Old Testament servant figure is _____.
5. Servant-hood is very special and high that involves a covenantal
    _____ _____ _____.

6. Jesus is the Servant portrayed in Isaiah 42:1-4. List four
    statements spoken in the passage that makes Him the example
    for all servants:
    a.
    b.
    c.
    d.

7. In the space below, explain the controlling Old Testament image
    of the servant/ master relationship found in Leviticus 25 and
    Exodus 21:

8. During a teachable moment with His disciples Jesus
    _____ their _____. The disciples were
    embarrassed. Why?
9. Jesus said, "You have only one _____.
10. Jesus said, "The greatest among you will be
    your _____."
11. As body leaders, we are called to Jesus' _____.
12. Jesus said, "I came not to be served, but
    _____ _____.
13. Once you know these things, you will be blessed if
    _____ _____ _____.
14. Sadly, today many Christians turn to the _____
    world to resolve _____ concerns.
15. Do you trust Jesus and His _____?

CONTRASTS IN LEADERSHIP STYLES

"If anyone serves Me, let him follow Me; and where I am,
there My servant will be also.
If anyone serve Me,
him My Father will honor"
(John 12:26).

You *must* be a servant, if you are going to be involved in God's work. We covered a number of Scripture passages from the Old and New Testament in the last chapter that described Jesus as God's Servant. He came as a servant to accomplish God's will in the redemption of humanity. Paul described Christ's attitude and commended it to us:

"Let this mind be in you which was also in Christ Jesus,
who being in the form of God, did not consider it
robbery to be equal with God, but made Himself of no
reputation, taking the form of a bondservant, and coming

> *in the likeness of men. And being found in appearance as*
> *a man, He humbled Himself and became obedient unto death,*
> *even the death of the cross"* (Philippians 2:5-8).

These verses present one of the most significant statements in all of Scripture on the nature of the incarnation, the fact that God became man. Also through this wonderful description of Christ, Paul clearly illustrates the servant principle of humility, "Let this mind be in you which was also in Christ Jesus:"

- All godly actions begin with the "renewing of your mind."
- Your right thinking produces right actions.
- Your actions are the fruit of your deepest thoughts.

Thinking and being like Jesus are requirements not only of the servant leader but also for the corporate body of Christ. Together we need to think and act like one being, like the Person of Jesus Christ. In (v. 8), note the contrast between Jesus' placing Himself in a debased status – as God the Father's elevation of Christ to a highly exalted status.

Service is not an option

Leadership in the church does not exalt – it serves. Jesus said, *"He who is greatest among you, let him be as the younger, and he who governs as he who serves"* (Luke 22:26). True servant-leaders labor for others, as a servant would. In short – the Lord's view of greatness *is* the exact opposite of the world's view. We have studied servant-hood in the person and teaching of Jesus. We will now look for it in the circle of His chosen.

In the context of the text quoted above, we have already seen just how entirely lacking in the grace of humility His disciples really were. At one point they argued about which of them should be the greatest. On another occasion the sons of Zebedee, with their mother, had asked for first place on His right and on His left. And later, at the table on His last night, there was again a contention over which should be accounted the greatest. This attitude was shown at other times as the power of the natural self would spontaneously rise up. The study of the meaning of all this will teach us a most import lesson in contrast concerning God's way and man's way.

"Not so with you!"

Certainly such incidents are the same today. We may find Spiritually-gifted people in all areas of the church, who like the disciples have fervent love for Christ, obey His commandments, and they have forsaken all to follow Him, yet they lack the grace of humility – which is mandatory for the Lord's servants who lead. More than a servant's heart is required. For those called to lead in the body of Christ; there is also to be the servant's leadership style and method. As I noted earlier James and John along with their mother left the other ten disciples very upset when they asked Jesus if they might sit on His right and His left in His kingdom. The displeasure of the other ten disciples was probably due to their own aspirations for such lofty positions. Jesus took advantage of this teachable moment and responded to them saying,

> *"You know that the rulers of the Gentiles lord it over them, and their high officials exercise authority over them. Not so with you. Instead, whoever wants to become great among you must be your servant and whoever wants to be first must be your slave – just as the Son of Man did not come to be served but to serve, and to give His life as a ransom for many"* (Matthew 20:25-28).

This passage of Scripture states it clearly, ***"Not so with you!"*** As we observe across the whole spectrum of the American churches, many violating or neglecting the purpose and commands from the Head of the body. When a person receives a very serious brain trauma, it renders the whole body immobile and sometimes rendered "brain dead." Why, because each member of the body relies on the head for its direction. Emphasis added throughout.

This principle is the same with the body of Christ, the church. In an earlier section, we saw that Jesus clearly declared that He is the Head of the body and there is "no other."

Secular versus Servant

- This can only mean one thing in the Church of God. Neither the pastor nor anyone else can take Jesus' place [the Head]. So rather than "over" like the Gentiles, [secular leaders style] – the [servant-leaders style] is "among." We cannot be servant-leaders if our position, role, or attitude tends to lift us above others and makes a distinction between us and the rest of the people of God.

Command versus Servant

- Rulers [the secular] "lord it over" and "exercise authority" over those they lead. They command or tell others what to do and demand conformity of behavior. But we cannot imagine a *servant* entering the house where he or she is assigned and begin to issue orders to those within. To use such authority in the church, one is calling for God's most serious rebuke, **"Not so with you!"**

Tell versus Show

- Secular command authority tells others what to do by issuing orders, and decisions the leader has made. The servant shows by example, not command – which is the primary way through which the servant leads behavior required [by example].

Results

- The command authority of the secular leader leads to behavioral change. There are many sanctions that secular leaders rely on to obtain the behavior they require – be they in the military, government or business. But the servants must rely on an inner response in those they influence. Without the power to coerce behavior, servants must seek the free choice of the one being led. Here is the key to the servant-leader's style versus the secular leader's style:

  1. The secular style achieves behavioral conformity.
  2. The servant style achieves heart commitment.

Power

- The secular leadership style has a wider range of corrective means to enforce response. In business, raises are denied, and many other symbols of approval or disapproval are used to coerce behavior.

- But in the church of Christ no such means of coercion are available. All such methods are decisively rejected!

There are many more contrasts in the illustration Jesus used. But the most striking and significant element of the passage is seen in the simple words: *"Not so with you."* Yet it is the servant style that brings victory. The servant-leader will bring the body into harmonious relationship and will lead its members toward maturity. The Lord Jesus Christ, the Head of the body, the church, will act through His servants to work His own good will!

**This measure of greatness is not position, power, or prestige –
it is service!**

Commitment to Servant-leadership

Commitment to servant-leadership carries with it a high cost. By forsaking the world's concept of leadership – the body leader is sure to:

- Be misunderstood
- Seem unimpressive
- Suffer under misunderstanding
- Be reduced at times to near-despair
- Be persecuted by peers

And it takes so much longer to gain heart response than behavioral conformity. The servant's gentleness itself, in a world where decisive and competitive men and women are admired, will lead to charges of weakness. Oh! But if he or she hold on to a total commitment to servant-hood and all it implies – the spiritual leader will be mightily used by God in the body and through his or her ministry Jesus will build His church.

STUDY SUMMARY: CHAPTER 11

1. You must be a _____, if you are going to be involved with God's work.

2. Scripture passages in both the Old and New Testaments describe Jesus as _____ _____.

3. In Scripture the incarnation is the _____ that _____ became _____.

4. All godly actions begin with the _____ _____ _____ _____.

5. Right _____ produces _____ actions.

6. Both the servant and the corporate body of Christ must _____ like Jesus.

7. Jesus debased His status as a man, while God, the Father _____ Him to a highly _____ status.

8. Leadership in the church does not exalt – it _____.

9. True servant-leaders labor for _____.

10. Explain in the space below the details surrounding the request to Jesus of the sons of Zebedee and their mother:

11. Explain in the space below the details of the phrase, "Not so with you!"

12. Rather than "over" the people like the Gentile or secular leader – the servant leader stands _____.

13. List three positions we cannot take as _____ _____ _____.

14. The servant leader always seeks a _____ _____, while the secular leader seeks a behavioral _____.

15. Total _____ is required of the _____ _____.

THE SERVANT'S ANOINTING

"I shall be anointed with fresh oil" (Psalm 92:10).

I n Old Testament times, the common believers had no anointing in or on them. The presence of God was in the Holy of Holies in the Temple. But God did anoint the king, priest, and prophet to stand in their respective offices. The Spirit of God would come upon these three servants of God to enable them to stand in their offices.

Anointing Today

In the last chapter, we expressed that you must be a servant, if you are going to be involved in God's work. Additionally, thinking and being like Jesus are requirements for servant-leaders and for the corporate body as well. It follows then that like Jesus we must be anointed for a special service or work.

In the New Testament, we see how the anointing was on the ministry of Jesus, and we can get a first-hand teaching about ministering under the anointing in Luke 4:14-19:

> *And Jesus returned in the power of the Holy Spirit into Galilee:*
> *and there went out a fame of Him*
> *through all the region round about.*
> *And He taught in their synagogues, being glorified of all.*

In verse 14 above, the word "power" is used in conjunction with the Holy Spirit. When we combine verses 14 and 15, we could say, "He returned in the power of the Holy Spirit and He taught," or, "He taught in the power of the Spirit." [For there is an anointing to teach].

> 16 *And He came to Nazareth, where He had been brought up: and, as His custom was, He went into the synagogue then on the Sabbath day, and stood up for to read.*

> 17 *And there was delivered unto Him the book of the prophet Isaiah. And when He had opened the book, He found the place where it was written,*

> 18 *The Spirit of the Lord us upon Me, because He has anointed Me:*

> - *to **preach** the gospel to the poor;*
> - *to **heal** the brokenhearted,*
> - *to **preach** deliverance to the captives,*
> - *and **recovering** of sight to the blind,*
> - *to **set at liberty** them that are bruised.*
> - *to **preach** the acceptable year of the Lord v.19.*[Emphasis mine]

Notice in conjunction with the Holy Spirit there first was the word "power" (v. 14) and then the word "anointed" (v18). Peter preaching to Cornelius and his household said,

> *"How God anointed Jesus of Nazareth with the Holy Ghost and with power: who went about doing good, and healing all that were oppressed of the devil; for God was with Him"* (Acts 10:38).

God empowered Him for conflict! He often seemed to treat sickness as an enemy. He was hostile toward it. Was this just adopted for Jesus' brief introductory ministry or should we not see Jesus as the revelation of the Father, perfectly demonstrating His will and purpose? In fact, Jesus claimed that the Father, dwelling in Him, did His works (see John 14:10).

In my estimation the gospels essentially reveal that God is for healing and against sickness. If Jesus, who was God perfectly manifest in the flesh, adopted such a position and spent so much of His time busily healing, why would we suppose that God the Father or the Son have now changed their minds?

Jesus enthusiastically congratulated those who demonstrated faith in Him. The frail woman, apparently hidden in the crowd, was happy to remain unseen and unknown, but Jesus found her and affirmed her: *"Your faith has made you whole"* (see Matthew 9:22). He enjoyed the opportunity to make public the faith that she had when she secretly touched His garment.

He showed the same enthusiasm when He marveled at the centurion's faith when he invited Jesus simply to "say the word" and not come to his home. Saddened that He had not seen such faith in Israel, Jesus expressed real appreciation for the fact that the Gentiles were beginning to put their trust in Him. This was in direct contrast to the unbelief manifested in His home town. Perhaps this is the shortfall with many pastors today, fear of failure prompted by unbelief.

Faith clearly plays a part in the release of healing. Notice what the following Scriptures has to say about faith:

- "Now faith is the substance of things hoped for, the evidence of things not seen" (Hebrews 11:1).
- "For we walk by faith, not by sight" (2 Corinthians 5:7).
- Jesus said, "He who believes in Me, the works that I do he will do also; and greater works than these he will do, because I go to My Father" (John 14:12).
- "For assuredly, I say to you, if you have faith as a mustard seed, you will say to this mountain, 'Move from here to there,' and it will move; and nothing will be impossible for you" (Matthew 17:20).
- Paul said, "My speech and my preaching were not with persuasive words of human wisdom, but in demonstration of the Spirit and of power, that your faith should not be in the wisdom of men but in the power of God" (1 Corinthians 2:4-5).
- If you will not believe, surely you shall not be established (Isaiah 7:9).

Faith is confidence that what God has promised or said will come to pass. Sight is an opposite of faith. If you can see clearly how something can be accomplished, probably faith is not required. One noteworthy evangelist said, "If you can see it just do it!"

Servant-leaders must always remember, your faith does not rest in a concept or an idea. Faith must be in a Person – God Himself! Faith is only valid in God and what He says He is purposing to do. If the thing you expect to happen is from you and not God, then you must depend on your own efforts and abilities.

Before you call yourself or others to exercise faith – be sure you have heard from God. With only mustard-seed sized faith in God, nothing is impossible. Jesus said His followers would do even greater things than He had done. Remember, our faith must be based on God's power and not human wisdom. Without faith it is impossible to please God.

I have often watched as faith grew in services or wherever people were being healed. On more than one occasion on Sunday morning after a brother or sister received healings, I have approached another person to ask what their problem was and they replied, "I had back pain, but I don't have it now." It's gone! While I was praying for someone else she believed the Lord for her healing. Many times others testify, "I've just been healed while you were praying for the others. I prayed for a lady who had returned home to die from cancer after the doctors had given up on her. She had lived in another State for many years, she was instantly healed. That was over twenty five years ago and she is still in the church witnessing and glorifying God!

Jesus said, *"The Spirit of the Lord is upon Me, because He has anointed Me ......"* (Luke 4:18). God anointed Jesus primarily to do two things according to this entire verse: to preach and to heal. [In conjunction with preaching, Jesus was anointed to teach].

The Spirit of the Lord is upon me

Today, because the local churches have been so redefined by cultural pluralism coupled with spiritual ignorance within; many people whose names have been on the church rolls for years, have no clue as to what God's will is for their lives. Observing this deplorable condition in the world today, they may ask, "Why am I here?" An old Catechism answer said, *"To love God* [be in right relationship with Him] *and glorify Him* [that He may manifest His glory in you and carry out His mission in the world through you] *forever."*

Jesus stood in the fivefold ministry offices listed in Ephesians 4:11:

1. Apostle
2. Prophet
3. Evangelist
4. Pastor
5. teacher

There are other gift listings found in the New Testament in First Corinthians 12, Romans 12 and other gifts scattered in some other New Testament books. All to which members of the body are called and anointed for service. The five-fold ministers of Ephesians 4:11 seem to be the pivotal gifts and those standing in these offices receive a special anointing. With the special anointing, you are empowered to better teach, preach, and do more. While you can stand in more than one office, you need find out where you are and; which one is your primary gift [also review pages 90-95 of this text].

Then God can use you, and you will exceed in your calling. God did not call us all to do the same thing, but He did call each of us to do something. No one is going to do it all. We need to complement each other, and if we will excel where our anointing is, we'll be a greater blessing to the body of Christ. I praise God for every minister and ministry called of God and anointed with the Holy Spirit. A variety of non-profitable actions are hindering the Spirit today among ministers:

- Many try to be a jack-of-all-trades
- Many try to do too much
- Many spread themselves too thin
- Many try to live by a combination of grace and law

All of these only lead to trouble. Trying to do something because someone else is doing it is very, very dangerous!

The Early church

Christians in the early church followed the directions of the Holy Spirit. Notice the testimony of the impact God had on their world:

- The disciples were filled with the Holy Spirit and spoke in unknown languages they never learned. Then Peter preached and "those who gladly received his word were baptized; and that day about three thousand souls were added to them" (Acts 2:41).
- God used Peter and John to heal a crippled beggar in the name of Jesus. They preached, and "many of those who heard the word believed: and the number of men came to be about five thousand" (Acts 4:4).
- God used Peter to raise Dorcas from the dead. "And it became known throughout all Joppa, and many believed on the Lord" (Acts 9:42).

Total dependence on God

From the examples in the early church, knowing and doing the will of God requires that each of us come to a total dependence on God to complete what He wants to do through you. Again, Jesus said our relationship to Him would be like a vine and its many branches. He said, "Without Me you can do nothing" (John 15:5).

When you are a servant of the Lord, you must remain within the intimate relationship in order to complete His work through you; depending on God alone. Notice in the following Scripture why you must depend on God to carry out His purposes. "I am the vine, you are the branches. He who abides in Me, and I in him, bears much fruit; for without Me you can do nothing" (John 15:6). When you abide in Christ:

- You change your worldview to be like His.
- You change your ways to be like His ways
- You listen and change your purposes to His purposes
- You experience Him carrying out His will supernaturally through you, when you listen to Him and obey.

Let the world see God at work, and He will attract people to Himself! Lift up Christ not in your words only – but in your life-living as well. That is radical reformation.

STUDY SUMMARY: CHAPTER 12

1. In Old Testament times, the common believers no _____ in or on them.
2. God anointed the _____ _____, and _____ to stand in their respective offices.
3. You must be a _____, if you are going to be involved in God's work.
4. In Luke 4:14-19, we see the _____ was on Jesus, likewise we must be _____ for a special service or work.
5. Jesus said, the Spirit of the Lord has anointed me to:
    a.
    b.
    c.
    d.
    e.
    f.

6. _____ clearly plays a part in the release of healing.
7. Faith is _____ that what God has promised or said will come to pass.
8. According to 2 Corinthians 5:7, we walk by _____, not by sight.
9. Servant leaders must always remember, their _____ does not rest in a _____ or an _____.
10. Remember our faith must be based on _____ _____ and not human wisdom.
11. Without faith it is impossible to _____ God.
12. God anointed Jesus primarily to do two things _____ and _____.
13. Jesus stood in the five-fold ministry as listed below:
    a.
    b.
    c.
    d.
    e.

14. Many of the other spiritual gifts are listed in the books of
    _____ and _____.
15. God used Peter to raise _____ from the dead.
16. Lift Christ not with your _____ but with
    your _____.

SECTION V

DISCIPLEING THE NEXT GENERATION

······················ CHAPTER 13 ····················

SAVING THE NEXT
GENERATION

"Train up a child in the way that he should go, and when he is old he will not depart from it" (Proverb 22:6).

For weeks the morning and evening newscasts have carried stories concerning football players at some point abusing their children [not disciplining, spanking, or chastising – but abusing]. Whether he used a small switch or a branch of a tree in chastening the child depends upon the perception of the reporter. On a December 13th newscast, it was announced that the President was asking for more than a billion dollars to fund beginning to educate children in daycares. While this may seem like progress to some, what it really does is expose our children to secular education [indoctrination] at the earliest possible time without actually going into the home itself to do so. If parents neglect this opportunity to bond and instill love and moral virtues in their babies, they won't get it. So the secularists and atheists stand ready to fill the void. The verse, Proverbs 22:6 above introduces one of the strongest biblical truths concerning parental child-rearing.

The Book of Proverbs, Deuteronomy and other Old and New Testament passages insist on moral training of the child by the parents or significant others in the home. The training must start immediately while the mind of the child is impressionable:

If you do not punish your children, you don't love them, but if you love your children, you will correct them (Proverbs 13:24 NCV).

Chasten your son while there is hope, and do not set your heart on his destruction (Proverbs 19:18).

Don't fail to punish children. If you spank them, they won't die. If you spank them, you will save them from death (Proverbs 23:13-14 NCV).

The greatest joy that parents can have is a wise son:

My son, if your heart is wise, My heart will rejoice – indeed, I myself' *Yes, my inmost being will rejoice when your lips speak right things* (Proverbs 23:15-16).

The father of the righteous will greatly rejoice, and he who begets a wise child will delight in him (Proverbs 23:24).

The most tragic sorrow is to have a foolish one:

He who begets a scoffer does so to his sorrow, and the father of a fool has no joy (Proverbs 17:21).

A foolish son is a grief to his father, and bitterness to her who bore him (Proverbs 17:25).

The foolish child is one of the hardest realities to face. There is no heartache so bad as the pain of realizing that one's child is a fool, indifferent toward God, and useless in life. The term son is generic – the central issue is not that he is a son or a daughter, but that he is wise or foolish. The child's behavior affects both parents. Both parents find their joy or sadness in their child who demonstrates skill in life.

Faith related parenting [The Way We Were?]

At the heart of the matter is an urgent need to find means of communicating biblical truth and lifestyles that promote moral maturity. Christian families are not as concerned with making certain God's Word is known and practiced as was the norm in former years. In doing so, we have failed:

- To prepare our children for moral maturity in decisions and conduct.
- To guide them toward completeness in Christ.
- Teach them a biblical worldview

However, numerous studies have found that the good old family altar [induction] to be an important means of encouraging moral development. Faith induction involves:

- Discussion of behavior expectations which have their roots in Scripture.
- Explaining reasons for standards.
- Discussing how they relate to God's commandments.
- Talking about internal matters such as attitudes relating to standards of conduct.
- Asking questions of the child that encourage reflective thinking.

This approach to parenting diametrically opposes dogmatic statements such as, "Good Christians don't act like that!" "As long as you live under my roof you will do as I say or else....!" I remember as a child, it was not uncommon to hear some parent threaten their child to be good; and if not this or that will happen to you – however there was no Scripture references to back up such threats, Then there were the guilt trips or just plain fear, especially of the boogy man, Satan. This produced an attitude of, "I'll be good in your sight or hearing to avoid the rod – but when out of sight and hearing, I can do as I please." Nothing of spiritual value was internalized from most of these confrontations.

God instructed parents

> *"And these words which I command you today shall be in your heart. You shall teach them diligently to your children, and shall talk of them when you sit in your house, when you walk by the way, when you lie down, and when you rise up. You shall bind them as a sign on your hand, and they shall be as frontlets between your eyes. You shall write them on the doorposts of your house and on your gates"* (Deuteronomy 6:6-9).

God instructed parents first to make sure faith is a part of their own hearts so that it naturally propelled them into a godly lifestyle. As they lived their lives, it was to be lived reflectively, integrating faith with life experiences. This integrative process was to be passed on naturally to children in a variety of situations common to daily living.

A number of years ago Christian parents desired that their children follow the teachings of the faith. However, even in my childhood the Word of God was taught as an external guide book – but few actually internalized the biblical truths which lead to conformity.

I heard a preacher tell this illustration: A father told his son to sit down, the boy continued to stand up, the father reached for a belt – the little boy sat down. He said to his father, I'm sitting down but I want you to know, my spirit is still standing up!

As was the case in the illustration, many people never learned to apply biblical principles to life situations. Therefore, they end up striving to do God's work while continuing to apply reason and other natural and secular solutions to the problem or circumstance.

Living Letters

The Prophet Jeremiah was concerned that Scripture become more than merely an external guide. Notice in Jeremiah 31:33, the words of God are recorded,

> *"But this is the covenant that I will make with the house of Israel after those days says the Lord: I will put My law in their minds, and write it on their hearts; and I will be their God, and they shall be My people"* (Jeremiah 31:33).

The Apostle Paul expressed a similar thought in the New Testament:

"You are our epistle written in our hearts, known and read by all men; clearly you are an epistle of Christ, ministered by us, written not with ink, but by the Spirit of the living God, not on tablets of stone but on tablets of flesh, that is, of the heart" (2 Corinthians 3:3).

The Corinthian Christians themselves were Paul's letter of recommendation. He did not need one because he already had one, the believing Corinthians and his ministry among them. Paul's love for the Corinthians was known to all who were acquainted with his ministry.

Thus, parenting communication of Christian beliefs to children when internalized holds potential not only for influencing spiritual growth, but moral judgment as well. Because of our vile society today; you may be thinking it is too late for this generation.

The parents should restore family devotions for the children's sake as well as their own. Unless something is done quickly; Satan will be in position to put America into a death grip – and therefore trap our children, grandchildren, and or great-grandchildren. Intercessory prayer works! It's time for the people "who know their God" to intervene for them – it's time to carry out great exploits" (see Daniel 11:32).

I am convinced that God is preparing His people for a final earthly offensive against the antichrist spirit. The antichrist spirit unleashed through ungodly people imbedded positionally in our institutions has dulled America's appreciation for the true God and the things of God. Our Christian heritage has been under attack for years, but the enemy was kept at bay because we had:

- One God, the God of Abraham, Isaac, and Jacob.
- A Christian consensus.
- Christianity was the benediction for the nation's agenda.

Immigrants coming into the country became Americans and for the most part were assimilated into the American culture. As a soldier for almost three decades, I was proud to be an American. As a Christian, I really enjoyed working alongside the Army chaplaincy and overseas missionaries while overseas, because other countries more or less had their own national religions [i.e. Hinduism, Shintoism, Confucius,

Islam and even paganism]. Today, it's basically the same as it was then in most of those countries, not very tolerant toward Christianity. Satan could not make any kind of headway against Christian beliefs in this country – so he has contaminated the beliefs of millions by promoting secular humanism while mixing in various tenets of foreign religions through multiculturalism [with its many gods]. Today it seems that all gods are welcome in the United States except our own true Creator, God of the Bible.

Satan has his allies in the public square literally cursing Christianity, because it is exclusive and cramps their lifestyles. Therefore, Satan would use education and secularism humanism to try to neutralize or obscure belief in the God of Christianity and the supernatural.

Humanism is taught to tens of millions of Americans through the public school system with complete freedom and exclusivity.

Multi-cultures bring with them many religions and many religions mean many gods and many different religious beliefs and influences. The education systems and curricula from kindergarten through college and university have been contaminated at all levels with secular humanism's agenda that fosters the destruction of Christianity, and the secularization of America. I've listed below just a few of the tenets of their Secular Humanism Manifesto:

- They claim that because they do not believe in God or the supernatural, secular humanism is not a religion.
- They believe that man is the measure of all things.
- They believe that humans are animals; and therefore are not responsible for their immoral behavior and other hideous actions.
- They believe that the Bible is man's invention.
- They have been at work secularizing America's society, government, public education, and media.
- They want the name of Jesus removed from the public square.
- They are trying to replace America's biblical worldview and Christian consensus with a secular multicultural worldview and secular consensus.[20]

I hate to think of what the alternative will be for America if we don't experience radical restoration. The true children of God must intercede for our children. It is obvious America is headed in the wrong direction. Things will get even worse as time passes. We have got to prepare this generation for the final hour. Each day our young people [ages 11-29] are a little more vulnerable and ready to embrace the deceptions of the antichrist spirit.

In past generations most young people were influenced through growing up in Christian homes, attending Christian churches and the Christian consensus, but strayed away from the church for a while – and then returned after marriage, college graduation or when they settled into a career. However, statistics reflect this is not the case with the present postmodern generation. As this generation is not returning to the church; their lack of Christian influence and moral standards have also been dwelt a deadly blow for them. If this generation was a patient in the emergency room of a hospital, it would probably immediately be rushed into the Intensive Care Unit, ICU!

Emergency response teams

Terrorist attacks, hurricanes, tornados, floods, droughts, famines wars and genocide, death and persecution of Christians have dominated the media for the past three decades. What will be the tragedies of the future? And how will the church respond? As a result many industries large and small and every government from the national level down to local towns and villages have organized emergency response teams. These teams consist of people with specialized skills to handle emergencies when and wherever they may arise. These individuals have a unique passion to identify and correct problems. Having a military background, I'm very familiar with the importance of this concept and need for having to use them in peace time and under actual combat conditions.

Most of the church is familiar with the concept; and have seen them in action [for example the Red Cross, the Baptist Men and many others through disaster relief for Katrina victims, the Haiti earthquake disaster, and even developing the mobile hospital emergency room].Yet, the Christian communities do not seem to be able to visualize the intense need for trained emergency response teams within the body of Christ.

A great percentage of church people experience personal problems and situations that just kind of wander around until someone comes up with a secular agency to refer them. One religious group sends out teams of people in various communities paying particular attention to the elderly. These teams repair windows, minor plumbing and carpentry problems, and winterizing and making homes safe, just to name a few projects they handle. Additionally a great percentage of people at the altar for prayer are never contacted. They come week after week! A trained and gifted team of altar workers would be able to respond to each person. Local churches have an opportunity to take responsibility and care for those in need. People are gripped with fears of some type of loss each day.

- It may be a loved one due to some type of crime.
- It may be loss of a job, a career, or property.
- Relationships are so fluid today that it could be the leaving of a mate after many years of marriage.
- The greatest loss are the millions of people heading for hell on a daily basis because Christians fail to see that this loss is very preventable, if we would rise up and do as our Lord has commanded us to do. Win them to Him! The tremendous loss of souls, who never experienced Jesus, far outweighs the loss of property.

When God's people witness the moral breakdown, spiritual decline of our churches and society; the very magnitude is mind-boggling for those without the church. However, what is being experienced with the present generation in the national culture – our spiritual adrenalin should begin to rise up! And those who are spiritually gifted and truly committed to the Lord's work should willingly move to the trouble spots within our particular space or area of influence and take action as you are guided of the Holy Spirit. Remember, the Lord has given the prescription for healing and restoration.

The Vision

I had a dream back in 1968. In it I was running in a desert place with a huge dust storm following me, right on my heels literally. However, it did not overtake or cover me, I saw myself down at the very base or bottom of the cloud running [just a little speck]. My pastor told me those clouds represented people following me.

I taught Sunday school, studied much and loved the Word. In 1970 I had my initiation into a teaching ministry in Colon, Republic of Panama, with a 16mm projector and films on the life of Jesus, Paul, Peter and others which I was able to borrow from the Chaplain's office. I partnered with a local pastor and we were on a mission for the Lord. People filled the church to watch the films. We had very little competition, because of the lack of televisions there. After the film I would summarize the movie, answer questions and fish for souls. The pastor immigrated to California and I ended up for a short time in charge of the congregation. A preacher native to Panama who had been living and pastoring for a number of years in Boston, Massachusetts came home and took over as pastor.

We then met and joined with Reverend Samuel Sellick and his wife Lydia, a Church of God missionary couple who pastored a Church of God Ministry to the Military, in the Canal Zone. Brother Sellick and I along with an interpreter went out into the jungle with those same old 16 mm films. I'd show the film then, Bro. Sellick and the interpreter would preach. Under the Sellicks my wife and I grew bolder and stronger in the Lord. I taught at the Christian center and when the denominational leaders came for a visit or tour from the headquarters in the States, I had to teach classes and workshops – they participated right along with the others. What a lesson and experience in humility. Only heaven knows the number of people saved during those three glorious years in Panama.

In 1973 we were assigned to Aberdeen Proving Grounds in Maryland, where we joined the Mount Zion Baptist Church in Harve De Grace, Maryland. We were interested in serving in the Christian Education Department. We were told that one had to complete Bible School before he or she could teach in the church. Off we went to school. Oh! What a blessing.

Over the next few years even though I was still on active duty, I participated in many seminars and conferences across denominational lines. In 1980 while assigned to duty in Seoul, South Korea, I was called into the gospel ministry. In March 1981 our pastor suffered a heart attack and though there were ministers senior to me; I was selected to be pastor.

This was a multicultural, multiracial congregation. The experience was invaluable further preparing Magdalene and me for future kingdom service. Since retirement from the military in 1984, we have served full-time in pastoral and teaching ministry. In an earlier section speaking on the world's servant and God's servant through whom He does the work – if we would just yield to Him. He can do great exploits through your testimony in your area of influence. There is room for all of us to be used of God. Are you a Barnabas? There are many more people through the centuries who have been used mightily of God and only heaven has a record of it. God needs faithful people through whom He can do His work.

Emergency repairs

In 1998, we founded the Bread of Life Ministries and Bible Institute with the express mission to come alongside churches and other Christian ministries to help train and equip the saints with the truth of God's Word to include teaching a biblical worldview. We were particularly interested in by-vocational ministers and others whose employment hindered or prevented their pursuing a traditional theological school or program. Additionally we chose to be a non-traditional and non-accredited institution so that we could waiver a portion of the pre-educational requirements for scholarship.

Though we have encountered several local pastors who accused us of usurping their responsibilities, many have embraced us and the Lord has used the Bread of Life to bless many people. Having been in the pulpit during the eleven o'clock hour on Sundays for many years, I had no idea of the reality that so many bona-fide Christians are moving away from the church traditions and others became sporadic in attendance in the institutional church.

In 1998 a Barna research indicated that some twenty million true Christians have left the institutional church for various reasons some of which are listed below. An updated report in 2013 revealed that number had grown to one hundred seventeen million. I will list some reasons for this condition that I have observed in the local churches today. This list is in no way all inclusive or in a particular order:

- Many churches are bogged down with many non-essentials; much of which does not honor or glorify God in all things.
- Many no longer practices "Love one another" as commanded in the Word of God.

- Many churches have abandoned or do not promote the Holy Spirit's Ministry [gifts and power].
- Many do not have a clear and posted mission (statement).
- Many do not teach and declare a clear statement of faith for all members.
- Many no longer teach [agape] love for God and neighbors.
- Many do not teach a biblical world-view for all members.
- Many do not obey the commission of soul-winning and making disciples as commanded by Christ.
- Many do not focus the relevancy of ministry and others are unwilling to accept change.
- Many are tired of too much support programming in the name of ministry.
- Many do little quality or relevant peaching and biblical teaching.
- Many do little or no local missions outreach to ["share the good news"]!
- Many do little to quell the many Cliché's and divisions in the church.
- Many do not take a stand on issues which are clearly biblically sinful.
- Many do little training and meaningful preparation of servnt leaders.
- Many do not practice "koinania" fellowship.

"If it is wrong fight it – if it is right fight for it!"
David Gibbs

From my personal observation another major cause for this shortfall is that many pastors and evangelists seem to be experiencing a reversal of roles. The pastors go fishing for souls at eleven a.m. each Sunday morning, while the evangelist comes along not with a soul-winning message, but a message focused to equip or edify the saints. Both are important to the church during this critical hour.

Incarnational transform [the hearts of people]

God created seeds to have within them the power to reproduce themselves. The Word of God [Seed] has the *ultimate* power to reproduce itself in us. Therefore, the truths of God's Word within the child of God have the power to reproduce themselves in the hearts of others. How does this work? God's leaders [servants] should touch the hearts of those they are called to lead; through their *power to influence* and *power to persevere.* Paul puts these two together when he says to Timothy,

> *"Watch your life and doctrine closely. Persevere in them, because if you do, you will save both yourself and your hearers"* (1 Timothy 4:16).

Life and teaching complement one another. Spiritual leaders are to lead others to a deeper commitment in Christ, the Head of the body, by modeling His example and the truths of God's Word that they teach.

Watch your life

Church leaders must "set the example" for the believers and watch their life closely insuring to display at all times Christian:

- Character
- Values
- Attitudes
- Behavior
- Faithfulness
- Loyalty
- Commitment

These traits reflect Christlikeness in them through the power of the Holy Spirit. Thus influencing and changing [transforming] hearts and attitudes. This is based solely on the character of the leader through the incarnational Word they teach. Notice, among those things mentioned as important qualifications of what God's leaders are to "be" – there is no mention of:

- Skills or training
- Titles
- Seminary degrees
- Ordination

- A particular spiritual gift
- Notable Ministries

Instead the focus is placed directly on the character of the leaders [what you "are"]. Paul referred to "the renewing of the mind" in Romans 12:1-2,

> *"I beseech you therefore, brethren, by the mercies of God, that you present your bodies a living sacrifice to God, which is your reasonable service. And do not be conformed to this world, but **be transformed by the renewing of your mind,** that you may prove what is that good and acceptable and perfect will of God."* Emphasis added.

His concern is that spiritual leaders realize this means more then "understanding." The Greek word *nous* encompasses the person's total outlook on life. This includes:

- Using our bodies to serve and obey God [in newness of life] (see 6:4, 13).
- The spiritual transformation of our attitudes, values, behavior, and beliefs.
- The spiritual transformation of our minds; and not conformed or molded by the values of the world.
- The spiritual transformation of a mind dedicated to God's truth will produce a life that can stand the test of time.
- The spiritual transformation of our minds begins with thinking soberly about oneself.

As our understanding of the body of Christ [the church] matures, our *whole approach* to leadership perceptions will have to be adjusted [from natural to the spiritual] accordingly. We must grasp the Scripture's assessment of the body as a *living organism* united to Jesus Christ, who *functions* as the Head.

In other words those recognized as leaders in the body of Christ are to be those whose lives publicly resist the temptations of our culture by allowing the Spirit to guide and shape a Christlike example through living out these truths.

Leaders in the body of Christ are selected on the basis of the kind of model – they are of what each Christian should be!

It is absolutely essential that the servant who would be a leader be this kind of person, because to motivate heart changes in others; this person has to be rooted in the incarnation of the Word that he or she teaches. Again, the basic qualification for spiritual leaders is that they be live demonstrations of the reality of all that they teach!

Watch your teaching

Today we attempt to communicate the written Word *only* in verbal form. And we are shocked as many believers fail to make the choice to obey the Word *and* put it into practice. To be effective, in verbal communication the truths must be *truly internalized* in you, and demonstrated through your incarnate lifestyle lived in the realities of what you have taught [we must live out those truths].

In our culture today a working definition of "teaching" is the imparting of knowledge [to the head]. Sadly that is the goal of many Christian communities. They settle for:

- Secularly prepared resource material
- Secular talents and reason
- A form of godliness
- Denying the ministry of the Holy Spirit
- Head knowledge over heart knowledge
- Born again and baptized, but have never developed an intimate personal relationship with God, their Father. They are content with belonging to the family of God and serving Him collectively with their brothers and sisters in the Lord whether that be by church attendance, Sunday school class, tithing, or even performing good works.
- This church certainly reflects the church of the Laodiceans in Revelation 3. It seems that the church had a combination of the weakness of the church of Philadelphia with the coldness

SAVING THE NEXT GENERATION

and deadness of the church of Sardis. Outwardly, they may be acknowledged as "good Christians."

EXAMPLE REMAINS THE BEST TEACHER

The question is – are they recognized as the sons of God? If not, their "religion" is vain *because it does not have the incarnational spirit within them that would reveal God's nature to the world.* Then there are those who are willing to pay the price involved in developing a personal relationship with the Father. Although God is pleased when a believer serves Him collectively with others of like precious faith, His ultimate desire for all of His children is that they come to know Him *individuality* and *develop* an intimate relationship with Him. Emphasis added throughout.

God wants His children to get to know Him personally so as they mature they will take on His nature and character – because this is what brings His manifest presence into our living and communicating [teaching] to others. Romans 8:14, presents an identifiable trait of the sons of God [sons is generic]: For as many as are led by the Spirit of God, they are the sons of God. Thus, one indication that teachers who *[watch their teaching]* are indeed the sons of God is the fact that they are led by the Spirit of God.

Sadly, most Christians do not have a clear understanding of exactly what this involves. To most church members when thinking of being led by the Spirit, they picture a particular brother or sister who often says, God told them to do this or that – and therefore they were compelled to obey.

Though having the ability to hear the voice of God and then act obediently on it is a part of what it means to be led by the Spirit – it is in no way all that is involved.

Being led of the Spirit of God implies not only that we are being obedient to the voice of the Spirit – but also developing God's character which will manifest in our persona, so that it's apparent – that we live out what we are living out [watching] what we teach to others. Being led of the Spirit therefore is twofold:

1. It is receiving instructions from God.
2. It is fulfilling the will of God in the character of Christ.

Truths that Transform

The Apostle Paul says in Romans 8:29 that God desires that the individual character of His children undergo a transformational process [teaching and practice] and become identical with the character of Jesus:

> *"For whom He did foreknow,*
> *He also did predestinate*
> *to be conformed*
> *to the image of His Son,*
> *that He might be the firstborn*
> *among many brethren."*

It is our Heavenly Father's will that His numerous adopted sons, be conformed to the image of His only begotten Son, Jesus. Being conformed to the image of Jesus simply means taking on His form: His likeness, His character and resemblance. When all of God's children are conformed to the likeness of His only begotten Son Jesus, then and only then will it become evident that they are led by the Spirit; and therefore truly are the sons of God. The whole of God's creation waits for that glorious day of revelation!

STUDY SUMMARY: CHAPTER 13

1. The Book of Proverbs has many _____ that insist on moral _____ of the child by the parents.
2. The training must start early when the _____ of the child is _____.
3. At the heart of the matter is an _____ _____ to find means of communicating biblical truth and _____ that promotes moral maturity.
4. In the space below, explain the reason for standards:

5. Ask questions of the child that encourages _____ thinking.
6. The approach to parenting opposes dogmatic statements such as:
   a.
   b.
   c.

7. God instructed parents to first make sure that _____ is a part of their own hearts so that it naturally propels them into a _____ _____.

8. God gave us His prescription for revival He said if we do four things:
   a.
   b.
   c.
   d.

He promised to do four things:
   a.
   b.
   c.
   d.

9. Revival is a _____ _____ of God's power.

10. The _____ spirit has dulled America's appreciation for the true _____ and the things of _____.

11. In the space below. Explain in one statement for any three of the eight tenets in the text:

    a.

    b.

    c.

12. From the text explain below how an emergency response team could be effectively used in the church today:

13. In the space below list three reasons why many true born-again Christians are leaving the traditional church:

    a.

    b.

    c.

14. Seeds have the power _____ to _____ themselves.

15. Paul admonished Timothy to watch his _____ and his _____.

CHAPTER 14

EQUIPPING THE NEXT GENERATION

We will not hide these truths from our children; we will tell
the generation about the glorious deeds of the Lord, about His
power and His mighty wonders (Psalm 78:4).

I t is so sad that the coming generations have such confusing
examples to follow as they observe their Christian communities
in America. There seems to be a myriad of ideas, gods, and
concepts; the majority of which are in error. Simply because the culture
from which most of their influence has rejected [without personal
examination] the only true God! The truth is found only in the Word of
God – in fact He is [Truth]. However, the Word or Truth of God is also
being rejected as just another among many.

It saddens me as I sit here working on this manuscript and thinking
of the many, many millions of people who are going to one day find out
the true truth – but it will be too late to do anything about it. My wife,
Magdalene and I were both raised up in the Baptist church with ties to

the Holiness Church for which I am ever grateful to God. Neither of us had any idea how those experiences would influence our destiny.

It has been said, "If you could mix together the Word of God from the Baptist and the Spiritual experience of the Holiness – the results would be one true believer."

The Christian culture in which we grew up [the 40's and 50's] was Old Testament oriented [thou shalt not], perhaps our generation was told a lot more "what was wrong" than "what was right." I'm sure this had a great influence on the very turbulent national culture of the [60's and 70's]. Having said that, that teaching was also foundational for our generations in that we went wild, but the convictions of our "law" oriented upbringing remained to rein us back in.

The cartoonists had a ball trying to define us with our "long hair" and "fro's." Some would feature our generation with upside down crosses, broken crosses, beads with great big crosses hanging from them, circled crosses on our everything – but crosses! Others depicted our generations with pictures of marijuana cigarettes dangling from our lips, and a swarm of fleas or flies circling our non-bathed bodies. It seems the cartoonists were trying to define the downward spiral of culture's sinful determination. Looking back it seems to have been an appropriate symbol of the brokenness in the American society's Christian consensus. Now you could do your own thing; which would soon manifest itself and change the very foundational stone of our society, the family. I'm sure Satan smiled upon it all, as segments of the media played it up to the max. Soon the imaginary line became blurred as the Ozzie and Harriet family model began to fade away.

A corresponding change was made in the Christian home at the same time. The family table was replaced by the TV. Soon not only the family but also the biblical worldview became questionable in the home, as the media began to encroach upon the individual minds and mindsets of family members. Soon the Saturday "shoot "em" ups" and the true story magazines, hidden everywhere imaginable were replaced with "love in the afternoon" [the soaps]. The blurred imaginary line has been erased, and the media and secular academia influences by now had conquered all [and has become god for many]. Considering what has been birthed in our society today, our "law"-abiding World War II era birth parents probably thought "little horns" were beginning to emerge from our heads in our generations.

The Post-Modern Family

The Huxtables came along in the eighties as the TV's model family. All resemblance of earlier generation's style of family life was all but gone. The mobile family on the run became the mainstay reinforced by the media. The family and the church became almost indistinguishable in the culture by the 90's. As the decades passed, very subtly the secular progresives and atheists have completed their one-hundred year move into the most influential institutional positions of media, education, government, and yes marriage and the family.

Today, a decade and a half into the new millennial they hold or influence most of the key institutional positions in our beloved country. Their secular agenda has been brought to the forefront, as recently seen in our justice system, as a single prosecutor, a single federal judge and a single grand jury usurped the power and will of "we the people" on issues already decided by the people.

Many of these ideologically influenced people are our children and grand-children, or other family members or friends and neighbors. Their aim seems to be the destruction of the United States of America. Since everything is relative in our society today and truth is up to the individual, so we are told; foundations are all but destroyed for a lack of godliness.

Connecting with the next generation

Chuck Colson was right when he said the church in America is three thousand miles wide and one inch deep. One problem is we don't know what the end product should be of all our doing. We need to review and restore what a true Christ follower looks like. What does Jesus have to say in the Gospels a disciple would be known for, and display in his or her life. It's possible you may belong to a church with a great number of young people, our job is to teach them how to feed themselves, walk on their own, find their place of service and reproduce in others what you have done for them. The church should never lose sight of the goal; and please don't underestimate the tendency of churches to get older over the years and become less effective connecting with the next generation.

No Christian would purposely hide the truths of Christianity from the next generation. But we do! Intentionally or not it's because of the concepts of our churches and ministries.

Many pastors have thrown their hands up and accepted the obvious, failing to reach young people – erosion that is impossible to stop naturally. I heard a pastor the other day refer to it as a virus. I believe it is possible to make the connection even in areas where young people have stopped or have never started to attend church. I believe that any church can make the connection – if the church would just be the church.

This generation includes the children [ours included] and young adults in our communities, many of them have little church background or experience. Making the connection to begin with requires an honest, soul-searching self-assessment.

The way we are

Unless a radical restoration as prescribed by our Lord, is adopted and implemented by the Christian church in the United States, the spiritual hunger of Americans will either go unmet or be satisfied by other faith groups. The world is changing in unprecedented ways. At the same time most of America's churches are sticking with programs and goals established by their founders in some cases as much as a hundred years ago. Many of the cures offered by the churches are like applying band aids to an open chest wound. Resistance to change held by many local churches far and wide is one major reason the Christian church, is experiencing such a deep decline in power and influence. Where is the church? Notice:

- People are desperate for *spiritual truth* – but it's hard to find in many of our Christian churches. New believers are not properly taught even the basic Bible truths, trained and assimilated into the life of sanctification. Their cry is *"Feed me."* Many leave the church within the first couple of months if we fail to meet this need.

- The church remains the nation's most segregated institution. This generation does not see race in the same light as their parents and grandparents. Many churches that integrate services are still segregated in their cemeteries.

- Though the church was called by Christ to care for the poor, ironically statistics show that roughly forty percent of the poor in the United States are children. A recent television newscast reported that Americans spend eight times more money on pets than missions of mercy. Young people need unconditional love and protection. They need to learn how to feed themselves and walk on their own. Their cry is *"Teach me."*

- Their primary need now is to find victory over sin and develop a life of godliness and obedience to Christ. They cry, *"Show me."*

- The young adults cry, *"Follow me."* Their primary need is to use their gifts in ministry and begin training others. You become co-laborers in the cause of Christ as our relationship upgrade to peers (see 2 Corinthians 8:23; Philippians 2:25).

- Technology and the mass media have forever changed the way we process information. However, most churches have yet to catch on to the new forms of effective technology and communications. We need to become "smart" like the computers, cell phones and TV's. Upgrade!

The main stumbling block we face

Christianity is having less impact on people's perspectives and behaviors than prior generations. Why is that? It is because a growing majority of people have dismissed the Christian faith as weak, outdated, and irrelevant. Speculation has placed the blame in many places, but the stumbling block for the church is not hiding – it's ever before our eyes. It is not the churches' theology, but it is the failure to apply what it believes in compelling ways:

- The church's downfall has not been the content of the message – but its failure to practice the truths expressed.

- Christians are their own worst enemy when it comes to representing Christ in the world – by not showing what authentic biblical Christianity looks like.
- Christian are also to show why Christianity represents a viable alternative to me-ism, materialism, existentialism, mysticism, and the other doctrines in today's popular culture.
- More and more of those who have turned to Christianity and churches seeking truth and meaning have left empty-handed, confused by the inability of Christians themselves to live the principles they profess.
- Churches fail to address the nagging anxieties and ever-present fears of the people.
- Many times the churches focus on outdated or secondary issues and offer shallow non-biblical or secular solutions.

Synthetic Faith

The practical irrelevance of Christian teaching has become profound. This condition coupled with the lack of perceived values associated with church life has resulted in a synthetic faith. Having been exposed to some basic Christian principles at times in their lives and perceiving all truth to be relative to the individual and his or her circumstances, Americans have begun to piece together a synthetic smorgasbord version of faith that borrows from any available and appealing faith; therefore:

- True faith revolves around God, His ordinances, principles and promises.
- The faith that catches the people's attention these days is that which *revolves* around the individual.
- A passive faith without Christ!
- Few Americans possess a sense of awe, fear, or trembling concerning God.
- The Holy Spirit and His Ministry in the church has been abandoned.

There is a Man in the glory, but it seems the church has lost sight of Him!

Political correctness is not biblical

"The fear of the Lord is the beginning of wisdom:"
A good understanding have all those
Who do His commandments
His praises endures forever" (Psalm 111:10).

Praise the Lord!
"Blessed is the man who fears the Lord,
Who delights greatly
in His commandments" (Psalm 112:1).

"Blessed is everyone who fears the Lord,
Who walks in His ways" (Psalm 128:1).

"The fear of the Lord is clean,
Enduring forever;
The judgments of the Lord are true
and righteous altogether" Psalm 19:9).

The fear of the Lord is an attitude of respect, a response of reverence and wonder. The fear of the Lord describes an obedient response of wonder, and awe before the Most High God. It is the only appropriate response to our Creator and Redeemer.

As I sat working on this manuscript, a couple of months back the announcer of the evening TV newscast seemed overjoyed as he stated that perhaps as early as tomorrow, the marriage amendment of one man and one woman voted in "by the people" of the State of North Carolina would no doubt be thrown out by "one man," a federal judge in Virginia who ruled down that State's amendment last week over the desires of the people. North Carolina is in the same circuit so the ACLU and other groups supporting same sex marriages were already celebrating what they considered a potential victory.

Rather than interpreting their sexuality through the lens of Scriptures, many people are interpreting the Scriptures through the lens of their sexuality.

I stated in an earlier section that when "we the people" is taken out of a nation – it can no longer claim to be a democracy. Perhaps many reading this would think I am offensive or politically incorrect with my comments. Notice how the dictionary defines politically correct: as conforming to a belief that language and practices could offend sensibilities (such as in matters of sex or race) should be eliminated.[21] There are many other terms and situations that have been added over the years.

Now that it has been taught and established in academia that Christianity is offensive and there is no God or Christ, notice the results. Sooner or later our sermons will be challenged for statements that the secularists consider not politically correct or by their standards offensive. Our young people ages 11-29 called Millennials have been especially affected by this ideology. Many in this group know absolutely nothing about God, Christ, and the things of God, because secular humanists in academia and other institutions have well indoctrinated them with their "no God" and "no supernatural" secular progressive agenda.

They have been taught a new way of thinking about all things pertaining to Christ and Christianity. Many of the truths that we were taught by our parents and Sunday school teachers about sin and its practices – as young people, we understood them to be wrong. Today's young people are being taught the same practices – though still sinful have been made legal or normal in society today.

Unless the local churches take a stand in a few years the congregation will be conformed to this ungodly secular worldview. Today many of the people in our congregations attend but won't join because they consider our biblical views as too narrow. They are considered narrow because they are the truths of God's Word – [without wiggle room]. No pastors or politicians are authorized to change the truths of God's Word for whatever reason they may deem necessary. In fact I heard a statistic the other day from a very notable researcher. He stated that in a survey of pastors were asked if they believed the Bible addressed the following issues abortion, same-sex, and other subjects a whopping 97% agreed that the Bible addressed these particular subjects. When asked if they spoke on these subjects, only 5% said yes.

Our congregations are sprinkled with cohabitating couples, and married people separated from their mates but not divorced, getting into relationships with other men or women as if they are single again. Many are good people and think they are alright with God. Today a great percentage of church members are suffering from biblical and spiritual ignorance. Rather than be silent for the sake of numbers, 501c status, or any other earthly reason – as children of God who know the truth, we must teach and act on truth rather than have people continue thinking that God approves of their immorality. God hates sin!

At 5:45 PM, October 10, 2014 a newscaster announced that a federal judge in Asheville had signed off the approval of "same sex" marriage in North Carolina by ruling the State's ban on same sex marriage unconstitutional. Sixty-one per cent, (500,000) people of North Carolinians voted for the amendment in 2012 [winning] to ban same sex marriage in the State of North Carolina and today one [person] a judge has struck down "we the people" once again.

The stroke of the judge's pen sent many pastors, boards and congregations scrambling to figure out how they were going to comply [compromise] with the judge's ruling in spite of what God's Word has said on the matter. It was reported in the news that the chief magistrate ordered that all magistrates across the State would comply and perform the marriages. One magistrate resigned immediately refusing because of his Christian worldview and biblical beliefs. One left standing! Many Christians either knowingly or unknowingly are allowing the culture to sway them against God's moral law.

Another set of un-biblical standards in the culture that's bleeding over into the Christian community are multi-divorces and multiple re-marriages. In fact a newscaster reported that you can now apply for a divorce on line. Some children are growing up with so many grandparents, that they really don't know any of them. Who is who?

These situations are fueled by prior generations failing to model the expected moral consciousness and truths of God's Word to the present postmodern generations.

Yet! It is not too late to do something about it. According to Scripture we can repent, turn from our wicked ways and pray – God's promises He will heal our land [of which these sinful generations are a part]. Pray for God's wisdom that you may become a wise counselor and intercessor in there for them. The Scripture says, "The fervent prayer of the righteous avails much!"

The communication gap

There is a communication gap between the generations which must be understood and dwelt with if we are going to save this generation. I personally know of several small churches that were at one time thriving with youth and young adults, but today there are absolutely no young people in membership or attendance.

We have five generations in the United States today. The names of these generations from the oldest to the youngest are:

1) Builders – born from 1927 through 1945
2) Boomers – born from 1946 through 1964
3) Busters – born from 1965 through 1983
4) Mosaics – born from 1984 through 2002
5) Digitals – born from 2003 through 2021[22]

A special note for Church Leaders: Those born from 1984 through 2003 [30 years old down to 11 years old] are commonly known as the "Millennials," a most critical group that requires *immediate* special care and attention if our churches are to save the next generation!

Each generation is unique and possessing its own identifying traits and global perspectives. The implications of intergenerational differences for ministry are enormous and too often ignored. A tremendous amount of reputable research has revealed that each of the generations view the world, spirituality, and the church differently from the others. The gaps in thinking and communications between the builders and boomers; the boomers and busters; and the busters and mosaics indicate that each succeeding generation is taking greater and greater liberties at redefining the faith.

Working with the Millennials [also called Generation-Y], ages 11 through 30 years old, you will quickly realize they are different from any other generation in history. They are fast rising due to the advances in technology and it is changing the way things are done. I accompanied my granddaughter to meeting of about thirty millennials. While they waited for the for the speaker I noticed there was only one person [me] in the room not doing something on their cell phone, texting, talking, games or something. Another observation I've gathered among them; their generation is used to being spoon-fed everything while those generations before them worked hard for everything they have. With my own grandchildren I hear, "Granddaddy I need so and so......." Whatever it is that they want, you can believe it's really a grant rather than a loan in their thinking.

I stated in an earlier section that winning the millennials is imperative if our local churches are to continue in the next generation. It is important that we learn more about the next generation in order to maximize our efforts to engage them spiritually. The relationship between millennials and the church is shifting and in critical condition – needing immediate attention! Barna research noted several helpful themes:

- The idea of finding ways to bring their faith in Jesus to the problems they encounter in the world.
- Helping millennials to understand their own mission in the world, through give and take dialogue with experienced leaders.
- Realize the one-way communication between the pulpit and pew is not how millennials experience their faith.
- Millennials don't want their faith just in Sunday worship, but holistic faith.[23]

Beyond the congregation

Beyond the congregation technology is also changing how Millennials learn about and discuss their faith. This generation is accustomed to foraging in multiple digital places at any given time – from texting to instogram, from news feeds to blogs and more. This digital deluge naturally includes matters of faith and spirituality. For example, more than four out of 10 practicing Christian Millennials say they participate in *online* conversations about faith and the same number say they blog or post comments on blogs about spiritual matters.

Technology provides useful tools, but we must be careful not to use technology as a substitute for relationship. Life is about knowing, loving, and serving God and other people.

STUDY SUMMARY: CHAPTER 14

1. Each church is potentially _____ generation from extinction.
2. Most American churches are sticking with _____ and _____ established by the founders many years ago.
3. People are desperate for spiritual _____ but it's hard to find in many of our churches.
4. Technology   and   the   _____ _____ have forever changed the way we process information.
5. The churches downfall has not been the content of the message, but its failure to _____ those _____.
6. The churches focus on _____ or _____ issues and many times offer shallow solutions.
7. Few Americans possess a _____ of _____, fear, or trembling concerning God.
8. When "we the people" is removed from our American heritage – we are no longer an authentic _____.
9. Christianity is having _____ _____ on people's perspectives and behaviors.
10. List the names and dates of birth for the five generations in the United States today:
    1.
    2.
    3.
    4.
    5.

11. Reputable research has revealed that each generation views the _____, _____, and the church differently from the others.
12. Each generation is unique and possessing its own _____ and global prospective.
13. Today's generation is used to being _____ fed.
14. Finding a way to bring their faith in Jesus to the _____ they encounter on the world.
15. We must never us technology as _____ for relationship.

CHAPTER 15

THE NEXT GENERATION'S SPIRITUAL CONNECTIONS

Remember those who rule over you, **who have spoke the word of God to you,** *whose* **faith** *follow, considering the outcome of their* **conduct** (Hebrews 13:7). Emphasis is mine.

Three times in Hebrew 13 the guidance of verse 7 is repeated concerning "them which have the rule over you."

1. In verse 7 – they are to be remembered.
2. In verse 17 – they are to be obeyed.
3. In verse 24 – they are to be saluted.

These are men and women anointed and appointed by God as channels through which His Word flows. We are not to salute them for their own sake, but for their works sake. It is whom [Christ] and what [the kingdom of God] they represent that demands our respect. They live godly lives and can be followed for their faith and example. The church desperately needs more people who embrace a deeper vision of the Christian faith.

We are on down the road after the turning point; and we must grasp these realities and respond in appropriate godly ways, as Christians, we are widely mistrusted by a skeptical generation of young people.

Young people are craving someone to mentor them. They want someone who will invest in their lives and show them the ways of the Lord. The churches' future hangs on the passing of the faith from one generation to the next through mentoring and intergenerational dialogue.

It seems that our churches are doing all they can to keep these generations apart. If churches are not careful time will take away their most precious resource, the seniors. Their most important need is to be needed. Despite what some are saying, research reflects that young people in the rising generations deeply desire older spiritual mentors who will guide them in spiritual formation and a deeper life walking with Christ.

World traveler Evelyn Christenson states that, Millennials feel that this generational gap is real, where parents have really abandoned them and almost abdicated their responsibility in modeling and teaching biblical values. Many believe their parents left them unequipped as they sought "the good life." So these young people are looking to the elders in the church for the solid moral and spiritual footing they have missed."[24]

Spiritual Examples

In 2 Timothy 1:3-5, Paul expresses the spiritual example in how Timothy's grandmother shared her faith down the generations:

"I thank God, whom I serve with a pure conscience, as my forefathers did, as without ceasing I remember you in my prayers night and day, greatly desiring to see you, being mindful of your tears, that I may be filled with joy, when I call to remembrance the genuine faith which dealt first in your grandmother Lois and your mother Eunice, and I am persuaded is in you also" Emphasis is mine.

In Titus 2:3-4, Paul expresses the spiritual example of older men and women should serve for everybody:

> *"That the older men be sober, reverent, temperate, sound in the faith, in love, in patience; the older women likewise, that they be reverent in behavior, not slanderers, not given to much wine, teachers of good things – that they may admonish the young women to love their husbands, to love their children, to be discreet, chaste, homemakers, good obedient to their own husbands, that the Word of God be not blasphemed."*

The character of those who are mature should serve as spiritual examples to all. Maturity is not determined simply by age or even by how much a person knows, it is determined by how skilled a person is in applying the truth of God's Word to life and in distinguishing good from evil.

Psalm 71:18 and Joel 1:2-3 also references how older generations were to impart the faith to younger generations. Despite obvious cultural differences, emerging generations have a deep God-given longing for connection with and guidance from those who have wisdom and experience beyond their own.

In Hebrews 5:13-14, the writer expresses the danger of those who are unskilled in the Word:

> *"For everyone who partakes only of milk is unskilled in the word of righteousness, for he is a babe. But solid food belongs to those who are of full age, that is, those who by reason of use have their senses exercised to discern both good and evil."*

The people to whom this letter is addressed did not necessarily lack the knowledge of righteousness; they lacked experience in practicing the knowledge they had. This message applies to the local churches of America as well. Maturity comes from the "practice" or "habit" of obeying the message of righteousness.

Our society is never without hope as long as families are properly shaping the moral and spiritual character of their children.

Mentoring ministry

A mentoring ministry in which smaller groups of individuals can be matched with those who are older is a great way to accomplish this. If your church is mainly young people, consider establishing a relationship with another church of mainly older people.

This would benefit both. Whatever it takes, the coming generations must work to establish mentoring relationships between older and younger generations. The passing on of wisdom must be restored to the church today. James said,

"If any of you lack wisdom,
Let him ask of God,
Who gives to all
Liberally and without
Reproach,
And it will be given to him"
(see James 1:5).

Scripture and the Generation

Individuals have the responsibility to *serve* their own generation.

It affirms the different natures of generations particularly that some generations are more responsive to the gospel than others. What is more, the Bible affirms that there is a natural succession of generations:

"A generation goes and a generation comes, but the earth remains forever" (Eccles. 1:4).

Notice how Homer compares generations to leaves:

> As the leaves
> of the trees are born and perish,
> thus pass the ages of man:
> old leaves to earth are dashed
> by autumn winds; others nurtured
> grow in Spring's living breadth;
> and the generations of man are so:
> one is born another passes away.

Each generation has an *evangelistic mandate* to communicate the good news to all generations.

Notice, the psalmist in Psalm 145:4 confirms,

"One generation shall praise Thy works to another and shall declare Thy mighty acts" (KJV).

Paul refers to David's service to his generation in Acts 13:36:

"For David, after he had served the purpose of God in his own generation, fell asleep" (KJV).

There is a responsibility to *teach* the next generation (see Psalm 48:13).

Faith Education

Sunday school has been the primary connection whereby people were taught about the Christian faith that conventional churches have with children until they reach adulthood. Today it's estimated that one in five adults claim to attend a Sunday school or Christian education class at a church during the weekend. According to research that figure has remained stable over the past two decades. Are you surprised?

During the past three or four decades, a new model of teaching/ instruction has emerged [small group ministry]. This popular trend is fast replacing the most common form of Christian education or discipleship training. The small-group models of ministry moves the people out of the four walls of the church; and into informal groups that usually meet in someone's home to study, pray, and interact. It has been one of the largest efforts of Protestant churches for more than twenty-five years.

True spiritual growth happens in the context of a vibrant Christian small group. In these groups everyone has the opportunity to participate. Discussions are open-ended to allow a diversity of opinions. The opportunity is afforded each one to be gracious toward others who express views that are different than your own. And more important is the opportunity to pray together and remain attentive to the presence of God speaking to and guiding the group through the Holy Spirit. In addition, you can get help for engaging in small group ministry by going to *SmallGroups.com* to find everything you need to successfully run your group.

Here at the Bread of Life Ministries, we have utilized the small-group/and house church ministry models for the past sixteen years. Like the conventional church, more women participate in small-group, but men are closing the gap. The concept has many advantages not afforded the average long established Christian church due to that old adage "we have never done it like that!"

Small Groups and generational communications

Having been involved with small groups for many years, I have been able to ascertain here are many benefits in the small-group/ house church. I will list a few that we enjoy:

- People come to the group seeking to grow spiritually [the fruit of the spirit]
- A statement of faith
- A clear mission statement
- A biblical worldview is a priority
- Kingdom-focused mission/ ministry

- Biblically-based teaching/ application [understood]
- More informal/ casual atmosphere attracts more men and young people.
- Married couples are attracted to the ministry
- One-on-one mentoring
- Holistic ministry is encouraged
- Participants' spiritual and physical needs are addressed
- Team ministry is encouraged
- Spiritual discussions
- Generational communications
- Practice "One another" ministering
- High rate of involvement among African Americans
- Clarification of spiritual gifts

If we are going to reach younger generations with the gospel of Jesus Christ, we must be sensitive to the seniors and builders. They will never abandon the traditional church, because to them there is no need of a radical change. In fact they are thinking, it took all of their lives to get it where it is.

One church I pastored for twelve years and I spent twelve years trying to institute change. Most of the older adults were not about to accept the new ways of experiencing and learning about God. It seemed as though I had two churches in one. Teaching, one-on-one and much prayer did not move most of the older adults to change in terms of values, perceptions, and behaviors at their advanced age.

Although it was a middle-sized church with quite a number of families, attracted many young Millennials, and young married couples, innovation was not readily accepted. Things would seem to be going well until the church meeting. Some of those matriarchs and patriarchs would undoubtedly try to coerce the young adults of how *they* expected them to respond to certain issues or don't bring this or that up, because it's too costly. Needless to say, we lost some of the younger people. I was not always popular with some of the older [builders] and even alienated by some fellow ministers.

We began a year-round *adopt a senior* program with the young people. The generations began to communicate with each other and needs were met on both sides. They even broke down the wall that had come between them and blended the congregation in worship. Praise God! Intergenerational communication is not a suggestion – is a "must have!"

The challenge to strengthen the existing form which they embrace, in a way that will enable every generation to grow spiritually is very important. Many of the issues that cause confusion actually are not that important and could really be dropped or revamped? Many viable suggestions, testimonies, examples, and biblical assistance are available at smallgroups.com.

STUDY SUMMARY: CHAPTER 15

1. Hebrew 13:7 warns us to remember those who rule over you, who _____ the word of God _____.
2. The church's future depends on our investing in the _____ of the next generation.
3. The _____ are the church's most precious resource.
4. The rising generations deeply desire older spiritual mentors who will _____ them in spiritual _____.
5. Evelyn Christian states that Millennials feel that the generational gap is real where _____ abandon them giving up their _____ is modeling and teaching biblical _____.
6. Older generations are to _____ the faith to younger generations (see 2 Timothy 1:3-5).
7. Family remains the _____ influence in people's lives.
8. Millennials are gravitating to churches where _____ and _____ is given top priority.
9. Each generation has an _____ mandate to communicate the _____ news to all generations.
10. The is a _____ to _____ the next generation (see Psalm 48:13).
11. A new model of teaching and instruction has emerged over the past three decades called the _____ _____ ministry.
12. The seniors and builders will never _____ the traditional church because to them there is no _____ of a radical change.
13. There are many benefits in the small group/ house churches. List seven in the space below:
    1.
    2.
    3.
    4.
    5.
    6.
    7.

14. Sunday school has been the primary connection whereby people were _____ about the Christian faith.
15. Some generations are more responsive to the _____ than others.

.

····· SECTION SIX ·····

RESTORE!

CHAPTER 16

GOD'S PRESCRIPTION FOR RADICAL RESTORATION

"If My people who are called by My name will
humble themselves,
and pray
and seek My face,
and turn from their wicked ways,
then I will forgive their sin
and heal their land."

(2 Chronicles 7:14)

I'm sure that few in America believe that we can fix this country through natural means. Therefore, we should all repent and return to God, our Creator. We need radical restoration and only God can do that. In fact God knew that we would be "here" at this moment in time before the foundation of the world.

God created us with a "free will" and He knows all about us. He knows that the greatest need for the church in America is radical restoration beginning with concept and worldview. And in turn through the people of God, He will heal the land. All knowing, He gave the promise in His prescription for a fruitful restoration of America to His people in the Scripture above.

He challenged His people – not the people that do not belong to Him – His people, the true Church [body of Christ] that "if" they would do *four things,* in His response He promises that He will do *four things.* The people of God *must:*

1. **Humble themselves** – that is to confess and die to self
2. **Pray** – that is to repent
3. **Seek His face** – right relationship
4. **turn from their wicked ways** – come back to Him

God promises that by their repentance and return He would:

1. **Hear** – from Heaven
2. **Forgive** – their sin
3. **Heal** – their land [America]
4. **Restore** – to the original [all that the devil has taken or distorted through deception on a large scale].

The Lord was appealing to His people to *intercede* for others in their prayers. We find a fine example in King Solomon's *intercessory* prayer during the dedication of the temple (study 2 Chronicles 6:3-42). He pleaded with God on behalf of the people and continued to pray fervently until the Lord answered. According to the Lord, this type of prayer will activate radical revival and restoration (see Daniel 9:19).

In His Word, God has expressed His will and prescription; and this is our only hope for the preservation and restoration of true biblical standards and moral values to save the next generation. If God's people – are willing to personally and corporately activate His prescription, God will heal our land. That's an inclusive blessing! We can and we must intercede for:

- Our churches (radical revival)
- Our homes (made godly)
- Our families (the biblical model)

- Our children, grandchildren and great-grand children (made whole)
- Our government (all levels)
- Our schools (all levels)

I realize that's a tall order. But God Himself has asked the question *"Is anything too hard for the Lord?"* (Genesis 18:14). The Lord will restore the Christian heritage and save America for the next generation. Restoration is a fresh demonstration of God's power. In an earlier section I talked about faith being about our attempting something that can't be accomplished without God.

Restoration is no more than a crop of wheat. Restoration comes from heaven when heroic souls enter the conflict determined to win or die – or if need be, to win and die! *"The kingdom of heaven suffereth violence, and the violent take it by force."*

– *Charles G. Finney*

Genuine faith only

Dr. Francis Schaffer was noted for calling truth, "true truth" or faith, "true faith" indicating that undoubtedly there is a counterfeit or false meaning being substituted for the true truth or truth faith. In recent years this trend has moved to the forefront of the culture. It is defined as "faith in faith" rather than faith in God – who is alive and at work in the world.

This trend has been nurtured by a recent wave of nonsectarian religious television programs, numerous novels, and nonfiction books that focus on a spirituality and a person's spiritual journey; however there is little or no reference to God the Father, Jesus the Son, or the Holy Spirit. There is another distinction here no, mention of the Christian faith.

Another challenging change in the cultural context is the position between belief and unbelief being identified as legitimate. Many of the proponents of unbelief came from among the leading intellectuals of their day; which included some members of the clergy. Our institutions of higher learning were among the most effective in advocating that belief in

God was a matter of personal choice – not a given for understanding the world in which we live.

The acceptance of unbelief as a legitimate option for every citizen and the new wave of faith in faith have radically changed the context for pastoral ministry from what it was in the middle of the twentieth century. That is one reason why it is much more difficult to be an effective pastor today than it was fifty years ago.

I see these proponents of unbelief and faith in faith in the same light as the others mentioned in earlier sections as antichrist.

People who pray want to pray. They are happy in being obedient and in calling on the name of the Lord. They have no faith in their faith. Their faith is in Jesus Christ!

Unbelief certainly negates true faith and therefore unbelievers cannot be counted as legitimate in true faith. The Scripture declares,

"But without faith it is impossible to please Him, for he who comes to God must believe that He is and; that He is a rewarder of those who diligently seek Him" (Hebrews 11:6).

The emphasis is on "He is" the true God. Genuine faith does not simply say only true God. Not believing that God exists is equivalent to calling Him a liar (see Romans 8:15, 16; Galatians 4:6; Titus 1:2; Hebrews 6:18).

In 1 John 5:10-11, the apostle John admonishes,

"He who believes in the Son of God has the witness in himself; he who does not believe God has made Him a liar, because he has not believed the testimony that God has given of His Son. And this is the testimony that God has given us eternal life, and this life is in His Son."

Radical Restoration requires Radical Faith

Will we have faith for the final hour? Ours is the hour for men and women of faith. It is my solemn conviction that the finest hour for the church is not yet. The greatest exploits of faith have yet to be done. <u>Faith is basic to all that we are in God and to all we can do for Him!</u>

In the Old Testament the three Hebrews had a radical faith. They cried, our God ..... *is able* to deliver us ..... and *He will deliver us.* Their faith went beyond being put into the fiery furnace. They had absolutely no doubt in God's ability.

As a matter of fact God did not choose to deliver them *from* the fiery furnace – but He chose to deliver then *in* the fiery furnace. They determined, at any cost, "We will not .... Serve your gods, nor worship the golden image" (see Daniel 3:28).

- Their faith had gone beyond the fire.
- Their faith believed when it could not see.

In the New Testament when prayer was made unto God without ceasing iron gates opened to the touch of an angel (see Acts 5:19). Today we have people who exercise radical faith rather than bow to the gods of this world.

When the chief magistrate ordered all magistrates to perform same sex marriages – one refused and resigned because to do so would violate his Christian beliefs. Hopefully there were more, but perhaps it's not in the best interest of our secular media to report it.

Radical restoration requires putting action to our faith. If we believe nothing is too hard for God, then as children of God we can go forth in faith and do great exploits not only in the church but in the marketplace, school boards, local political offices, the nation's classrooms and industry.

Our society is overwhelmed with fear and anxiety today. Leaving conditions and problems up to the politicians has netted very little, especially when that person has to be concerned with public opinion and re-election. Faith honors God, and God honors faith and goes wherever faith takes Him. True biblical faith, can do to the glory of God all that God can do, because true faith won't ask amiss.

> *"Now this is the confidence that we have in Him, that if we ask anything according to His will, He hears us. And if we know that He hears us, whatever we ask, we know that we have the petitions that we have asked of Him"* (1 John 5:14-15).

The key to *knowing* that God hears our prayers is to pray according to His will!

To pray according to God's will is to pray in accord with what He would want, not what we would desire or insist that He do for us (see John 14:13, 14). John has already said that answered prayer also depends on *obedience* to God's commandments and *avoiding sin* (see John 3:21; Psalm 66:18; John 15:7; 1 Peter 3:7).

Since true believers:

- Know God's Word [His will]
- Practice those things that are pleasing to Him,
- Never insist on your own will,
- But supremely seek God's desires
- Know that God always hear the prayers of His children – but not in the same manner they were presented to Him (see Matthew 26:39-42).

One great value of reading the Word of God is that it is faith-feeding, for "faith comes by hearing, and hearing by the Word of God" (Galatians 3:5).

Hindrances to radical restoration

There are many hindrances to restoration. The Scriptures speak of two major hindrances toward the Lord's will, religious traditions and unbelief.

Religious Traditions

The Pharisees were criticizing Jesus for allowing His disciples to break Jewish tradition by not washing their hands before they ate. Jesus rebuked them for being so obsessed with traditions that they failed to observe *basic commandments.* They were so concerned with external ceremonial washings and dietary regulations that they failed to *deal with character.*

> *"Thus you have made the commandment of God of no effect by your tradition .... And in vain you worship Me, teaching as doctrine the commandments of men"* (Matthew 15:6, 9).

Jesus' words apply to all of us. We are to be good stewards of personal finances and possessions. Likewise, we are to be good stewards of the material assets in our churches. But if we focus on "things," no matter how much they mean to us, so that we become distracted from the eternal – we have lost our focus and forfeit our true purpose for being.

Unbelief

To not believe the truth of God's Word means unbelief. It never fails to amaze me, the number of people who will tell you they believe the Bible is truth; and they don't believe the media. However, they spend hours each day reading newspapers and listening to biased television and radio newscasts.

Though they believe the Bible is God's truth – they spend only a fraction of their time in the Bible as compared with that spent with the media. Non-believers express their unbelief in one or all three types below:

- *Ignorance* – I don't know God. I've never heard of Him.
- *Wrong teaching* – I don't believe in miracles. I was taught that miracles ended when the last apostle died. Some are even taught that miracles are of the devil.
- *Natural thoughts* – It is God's will that I be sick. I prayed, and when I went back to the doctor my illness had grown worse.

Example is the way

It is interesting to note that the disciples did not request, "Lord teach us to preach." They had often heard Jesus preach; they had seen His success; they had seen Him handle the crowds. Yet they did not seek to be taught His methods – but to learn His secret. They wanted to know His way of access to God, and thus they said, "Lord teach us to pray." They saw by His example; that example is the only real way to teach. It is one thing to instruct people about prayer – but it is quite another thing to pray. The same is true concerning teaching sacrifice and "death to self."

EXAMPLE IS THE ONLY REAL WAY TO TEACH.

In reality other than example everything else is philosophizing, counselling and instructing. Christ taught His disciples to pray, but He also led the way to the altar.

The disciples knew He had success in prayer by the answers He got. God seeks someone *"to stand in the gap."*

- We want to be clothed with power – God wants to strip us.
- We want power – God wants to expose our weakness.
- We want large dividends for small investments of prayer.

In this postmodern age people want to submit microwave pop up prayers; expecting instant answers. **But God says, *"Wait on the Lord …….. and He will strengthen your heart."***

Standing in the Gap

> *"So I sought for a man among them who would make up a wall, and stand in the gap before Me on behalf of the land, that I should not destroy it; but I found no one"* (Ezekiel 22:30).

God could not find a spiritual leader to guide the people in godliness. Why not? Apart from Jeremiah and Ezekiel who were faithful to God, there was not a man in Israel capable of advocacy for the nation when its sin had gone so far. No one could lead the people into *repentance* and draw Israel back from the judgment that came in 586 B.C. (see Jeremiah 7:26, 36; 19:15).

Only Jesus Christ, who is God Himself, will have the character and the credentials sufficient to do what no one can do, *intercede* for Israel (see Isaiah 59:16-19; 63:5; Revelation 5). Christ was *rejected* by them in His *earthly ministry; therefore the effects of this judgment continues* today until they turn to Him in faith (see Zechariah 12:10; 3:1).

In Ezekiel 3:17 God informs Ezekiel that He has made him a *watchman* for the house of Israel. This role was *spiritually* analogous to our role as watchmen in the military. Standing vigilant to spot the approach of an enemy and warn the residents to execute a defense. The prophet gave timely warnings of approaching judgment. Notice the work of a watchman.

When I entered the Army in 1958, as young soldiers we had to pull prison chaser duty and guard. I don't know whether it was true or not, but we were told if the prisoner escaped – we would have to complete the prisoner's sentence. We didn't know whether it was true or not. Not one prisoner escaped during our watch! In those days allowing any breach of the perimeter during your watch could have meant death. The recent breaches of the Whitehouse fence would have meant certain death for those who dared to try such a thing in our day.

Again the word of the Lord came to me saying, Son of man, speak to the children of your people, and say to them: When I bring the sword upon the land, and the people of the land take a man from their territory and make him their watchman, **when he sees the sword coming upon the land, if he blows the trumpet and warns the people, then whoever hears the sound of the trumpet and does not take warning, if the sword comes and takes him away, his blood shall be on his own head. He heard the sound of the trumpet, but did not take warning; his blood shall be upon himself.**

But he who takes warning will save his life. But if the watchman sees the sword coming and does not blow the trumpet, and the people are not warned, and the sword comes and takes <u>any</u> person from among them, he is taken away in

his iniquity; but his blood I will require at the watchman's hand (Ezekiel 33:1-6).

So you, son of man: I have made you a watchman for the house of Israel; therefore you shall hear a word from My mouth and warn them for Me. When I say to the wicked, 'O wicked man you shall surely die!' and you do not speak to warn the wicked to turn from his way, that wicked man shall die in his iniquity; but his blood I will require at your hand. Nevertheless if you warn the wicked to turn from his way, and he does not turn from his way, he shall die in his iniquity, but you have delivered you soul (vv. 7-9). Emphasis added.

A watchman who sounded the warning of repentance for sin was not to be judged. But the one who failed to deliver the message was held accountable. This referred to unfaithfulness on the part of the watchman for which he bore responsibility and was chastened by God.

Why won't they listen?

As the people of God, each of us are called to be watchmen for the Lord; and as Ezekiel was called to watch over Israel; as believers we are called to warn and watch over America, beginning with our own family and others in our areas of influence. From a human perspective we need to diligently attempt to convince people of the truth of God's Word, using explanations that make sense to them. Over and over again the prophets, apostles, and Jesus Christ Himself warned and called upon people to come to God in repentance. The word "repentance" literally means "to change one's mind."

STUDY SUMMARY: CHAPTER 16

1. In 2 Chronicles 7:14, God challenged His people to do four things and He promises to do four things to heal their land. As the people of God – we have His prescription for healing America:

They were to:
a.
b.
c.
d.

In turn He will:
a.
b.
c.
d.

2. Is anything too _____ _____ God?
3. Unbelief negates _____.
4. _____ is basic to all we are in God.
5. The key to knowing that God hears our prayers is to pray in _____ His _____.
6. Good behavior can be learned through force or coercion, but godly character is developed in a _____ of live.
7. Unlike the gifts of the Spirit which are give, the fruit of the Spirit must be _____ and _____.
8. King Solomon was a good example for _____ prayer in 2 Chronicles 6:3-4.
9. If God's people are willing to personally and corporately activate His _____ He will heal the land [Home, Church, America].
10. Another challenging change in cultural context today is the position between belief and _____.
11. Not believing God is the same as calling Him a _____.

12. The key to knowing that God hears our prayers is to
_____ His _____.

13. Non-believers normally express their unbelief in the following
three ways:
    1.
    2.
    3.

14. As Ezekiel was called by God to be a watchman for Israel,
the people of God are called to _____ and pray
for _____.

15. Example is the only _____
way to _____.

CHAPTER 17

WHY THEY WON'T LISTEN

"As a man thinks in his heart so is he" (Proverbs 23:7)

Today our politicians and many church leaders as well stare blindly into the crystal ball of human diplomacy, in the midst of stealthy humanistic philosophies, while this postmodern mostly un-churched generation speeds headlong down the destructive atheistic paths of secular humanism.

The ultimate goal of humanism is that no personal qualities, emotions, or desires are to be valued – only productivity. To achieve this people would have to be incorporated into a mass social structure to produce more of what they are – matter. This is considered the ultimate destruction of created order with inherit value and relational purposes.

Secular humanism is a tenet of naturalism, which *conveniently* claims the non- existence of God or the supernatural – and therefore not considered a religion. Though they claimed to be when they started out. So without God – man becomes the measure of all things. All at a crucial time when the moral laws of God and the name of Jesus are being trampled into the dust of public opinion which follows the lead of the secular media and academia. What was known only as theory such as "evolution," "natural selection" "survival of the fittest" and the belief that humans are animals when I was in high school back in the 50's has not only taken over the present generation as truth – but touting itself as the only truth. Christianity and Creation were accepted throughout as truth with very few questions asked. Today there has been a subtle reversal of roles. Christianity and Creation are being promoted as non-truth or just another religion at best, while humanism is being swallowed hook, line, and sinker as the *only* truth.

Enters the Lizard

Birthed in academia through such notable educators as John Dewey who referred *to humanism* as a *Common Faith,* advocated an ecumenical belief system based in humanistic values comparable with his views of ethics and biology.[25] And his contemporary Charles Francis Potter who authored, *Humanism: A New Religion,* which stated the movement's objective to replace a theistic religion with an atheistic one.

His thesis, considered education to be Humanism's most powerful ally, every American public school is a school of Humanism. He surmised that theistic Sunday schools, meeting one hour a week, and teaching only a fraction of the children had no chance against a five-day program of humanistic teaching. [26]

The proof is certainly in the pudding! When the time was right – with secular allies in the court system when religion became burdensome to their objectives, it was dropped. Sometimes as I sit here working on a manuscript, I see a brown lizard outside on the windowsill, when something threatens its path, it quickly drops into the green foliage below at the same time changing its color to green blending in so well that you really have to look close to see it. In fact unless you know it's there and know where to look you will probably miss its very existence. That's what secular humanists did through the First Amendment to free themselves of religion [the lizard affect].

The end result of secular humanism no longer being a religion is that humanism has been taught to untold millions of Americans through the public school system *(for decades)* with *complete freedom and exclusivity.* What does this equate to? Humanism's values have been so permeated into every facet of society to the end that *we have become unconscious of them!* Emphasis added.

Though no longer claiming to be a religion, humanism has become the very essence of religious culture – that the adherents of a particular culture take the *fundamental beliefs to be self-evident.* Here is the satanic punch line in humanism: **whatever-it-is seems the only way to be!** While education is humanism's means of transporting its beliefs and creeds, materialism is the money that moves it throughout the culture.

Since the days of Dewey and Potter, secularists have been working feverously to erase any and all traces of God from society. Listen to any newscast or read any daily newspaper and I'm sure you will see some form of discrimination against Christianity, it may be an innocent child with a New Testament in his or her backpack at school or someone saying a word for the Lord in a public meeting. On yesterday's national news a fire chief was fired for expressing his Christian beliefs concerning same-sex marriage. Without repeating, I spoke of other examples in an earlier section. Another big satanic deception today is the so-called separation of church and state. Think about it, how can there possibly be a separation of church and state when God owns both of them?

Enter bluffs and smokescreens

There is a saying, "We've been wrong so long, when right comes along we kill it. Why? Because by humanistic standards, we've reached a point where wrong seems "the only way to be." Certainly this has had a great negative effect on the church. As a pastor, I've noticed that even having been taught rightly concerning godly stewardship, financial support for churches is down along with attendance. Many of our people are opting out for larger houses, luxury cars and designer clothes. Truthfully as a result of our senior generation's exit, some things you'd never expect are coming to past. I use to think that you would never see a for sale sign in front of a church due to foreclosure. Today it has become common place. Many churches across the country are deteriorating from lack of use, while others are put to other uses. In a town close to where I pastor, right on main street one of the town's landmark churches has a large for sale sign out front. There are not too many other uses for many of these structures. I am also seeing many young adults who have been consumed with materialism striving to continue to embrace their Christian beliefs, but eventually giving up for a job to pay for their "stuff."

Earlier I spoke of the tension between the biblical worldview and the secular or materialistic worldview. The danger here lies in people embracing the materialistic worldview because material reality to them is the only reality there is. It is important that we make a distinction between a materialistic person and a materialistic worldview.

Up above I described the materialistic person who let "stuff" become more important to them than anything else. The danger of the materialistic worldview though bears repeating again and again: it teaches: *that a materialistic worldview is one in which a material reality is the only reality there is.* That worldview is able to permeate the whole culture because the church is not teaching and providing a biblical counterculture. Something to think about: the secularists have taken the Ten Commandments and prayer out of public schools and replaced them with a policeman in the hall.

The millennial generation was born into this materialistic worldview. So secular humanism has reached one of their goals of getting a generation to collectively accept their standard that defines worth based solely on what they can see or touch or buy or sell – this is much, much worse! Are you upset!

Only Humans

Jesus said, "Without Me you will do anything." How did we get to this place? First of all without Him we are separated from our created purpose. We simply become humanistic machines acting out the motions of life, while really we have no life. So our search for purpose begins in our surroundings – in those things that make up our lives.

A feeling of despair sets in, so we think the answers lie in something outside of us. As we gaze outward we only get a reflection back of whatever hollow things we look to. Because we can find no meaning in anything but the One who gave it to us. We widen our search farther away, different cities, different partners; different paths hoping that one will lead us to the "other" we are looking for. We even look in the wrong places, which is so common to happen whenever people reject God.

According to Romans 1:21-23, the next step after rejecting God is turning to vain thinking and foolish reasoning which reverts them from the truth to lies. Next come idolatry, honoring the creature [man] rather than the Creator:

People replaced God's truth with Satan's lie. What is his lie? They began to worship the creature instead of the Creator, worship man instead of God, worship things instead of Christ. Satan tempted Jesus to do this (see Matthew 4:8-11).

The truth believed and obeyed sets us free, but the truth rejected and disobeyed makes us slaves (see John 8:31-32). Has America reached the lowest level of their downward spiral: they do not even want to have knowledge of God! "The fool has said in his heart, "There is no God" (Psalm 14:1).

It is sad to see the tragic results of this decline in America's culture. Evolutionists, an arm of secular humanism wants us to believe that humans have "evolved" from primitive, ignorant, beast-like forms into what they are today. Paul says just the opposite: man began the highest of God's creation, but he made himself into a beast by choice! Notice the three judgments of God as a result:

- God gave them up to uncleanness and idolatry (vv. 24-25).
- God gave them over to vile passions (vv. 26-27).
- God gave them over to a reprobate mind (v. 28).

God gave them up! This is the revelation of God's wrath (see v. 18). This vile list of sins is practiced today around the world with the approval of society. People know that sin will be judged, yet they take pleasure in it anyway. From Romans 2:1-3:8, Paul looking at his own people makes sure they understand that they are equally condemned with the Gentiles and are without excuse.

The same two "excuses" that the Jews used in Paul's day are still making their rounds today:

1. "I am better than others, so I don't need Christ."
2. "God has been good to me and will certainly never condemn me."

But don't be deceived, God's final judgment will not be according to peoples' opinions and evaluations it will be according to truth. God wants faithful, mature watchmen [the word is generic] to carry His message of repentance and salvation to the world and intercede for others. We must stand and not falter!

STUDY SUMMARY: CHAPTER 17

1. The ultimate goal of humanism is that no _____ _____ _____ or desires are to be valued.
2. Humanism only values _____.
3. Secular Humanism is a tenet of _____.
4. Humanism claims that without God _____ is the measure of all things.
5. _____ is being promoted as the only _____.
6. Humanism's most powerful ally is _____.
7. Every public school in America is a school of _____.
8. For decades humanism has been taught in public school systems nationwide. Untold millions have been _____.
9. Humanism's values have so permeated every facet of society to the end that we have become _____ to them.
10. What is humanism's punch line? Explain in the space below.
11. _____ owns church and state.
12. In the space below explain the tension between the biblical worldview and the materialistic worldview.
13. Humanism is transported by _____.
14. Humanistic judges in our courts is taking the _____ from the people.
15. Briefly explain in the space below the three aspects of Satan's lie.

CHAPTER 18

HISTORY OF THE RESTORATION [CONTINUES]

And it shall come to pass in the last days, says God,
That I will pour out My Spirit on all flesh;
Your sons and your daughters shall prophesy;
Your young men shall see visions,
Your old men shall dream dreams.

Acts 2:17

Repent therefore and be converted, that your sins may
be blotted out, so that times of refreshing may come from
the presence of the Lord, and that He may send Jesus
Christ, who was preached to you before, whom heaven
must receive until the time of restoration of all things,
which God has spoken by the mouth of all His
holy prophets since the world began.

Acts 3:19-21

I n the last days, we will experience a time of refreshing restoration as a result of genuine repentance; which precedes the return of the Lord Jesus Christ, according to the Scripture. This can occur only after the restoration of all things. The word restoration signifies returning something to the state in which it first began. If something is restored, it is because it has deteriorated from its original condition or that it has simply been neglected to the point of its destruction.

Restoration, then, is the process of correcting a condition through a process of change.

Scripture shows that when God restores things they surpass their original condition. When God restored to Job that which Satan had taken from him, He blessed him with double of that he had lost. The prophet Isaiah described the people of God as "robbed and plundered, snared, hidden, and prey" (see Isaiah 42:22). It seems he is talking about the church today. This passage ends with a mandate from God's throne, "Restore!" The sovereign God chooses to involve His church in His purposes and eternal plans:

- "For we are God's fellow workers ...." (see 1 Corinthians 3:9).
- "….. Of all that Jesus began to do and teach …." (see Acts1:1-4).

Throughout history, beginning with Adam and Eve's sin in the Garden of Eden, which was passed on to all future generations, the Lord has been *restoring all* that the enemy has stolen through deceits and false philosophies based on the traditions of man and not on Christ!

Upon His return to heaven, Jesus Christ left with His people the creative power of the Holy Spirit. The outpouring of the Holy Spirit on the day of Pentecost gave His people the anointing as Jesus' ambassadors throughout the world. Additionally, as stated earlier in Chapter 12, He gave five ministerial gifts to His Church to spread throughout the world and establish the kingdom of God here on earth by saving the lost and destroying the works of Satan.

The Church in the early years

During the first five hundred years of the church, false doctrines infiltrated it, trying to slowly sink and destroy it. Very subtly these erroneous doctrines robbed the church of the five ministerial gifts and the spiritual gifts. The leadership of the church fell into apostasy and collaborated with the Roman government, departed from the apostles' doctrine and precepts of the faith handed down by the Church fathers. The apostle Paul refers to these as:

- Shipwrecks concerning the faith (1 Timothy 1:1-19)
- Men of corrupt minds, disapproved concerning the faith (1Timothy 3:3-8).

Other actions through the passing of years:

- The manifestations of the Holy Spirit were removed from the church and could not be taught.
- The church eliminated the ministries of the apostle, then the prophet, the evangelist, and the teacher.
- This process resulted in the establishment of an ecclesiastical hierarchy *very different* from that established by Christ and by the apostles.
- The doctrines of man began to have more authority than the Word of God.
- The church was dead without life.

Nevertheless, God has always kept a faithful remnant, that in God's own time *(kairos)* stood up to bring changes and reforms that conform to the Word of God and its doctrines.[27]

The Protestant Reformation

The Protestant Reformation of the sixteenth century ignited a spiritual restoration that shook the world. Entire communities were transformed by the power of this *new* revelation of the grace of God. Church history teaches us that in the year 1715 through a Catholic priest named Martin Luther, God began to *restore* the lost truths of God's

Word. This was a *radical restoration* of truth instituted by the Holy Spirit to rescue, correct error, and strengthen the church. Emphasis added.

Think about it, the Protestant Churches came into existence because Martin Luther and numerous other ministers broke away from the Catholic Church and Catholicism. Having received revelation of truth it became impossible for him to continue in the religious system that he believed was in error to the Word of God.

Denominations

Protestantism came into existence because the Holy Spirit initiated the period of restoration of the church. The Protestant Churches [Denominations] brought back into the church the revelation, proper application, and reestablishment of the first doctrine of Christ – *repentance from dead works.*[28]

Today concerning denominations, we hear that they are old and obsolete; and phrases like post-denomination or post Christian era are commonly heard even among some church leaders. Many of our young independent churches are trying to distance themselves from denominations. In doing so they are ignoring the fact that God used denominations mightily in the restoration process of:

- Restoration of the gospel of Christ
- Restoration of the foundational truths of the gospel of Jesus Christ.
- Restoration of eternal life.
- Restoration of the faith once delivered to the saints.
- Restoration of the Trinity [Father, Son, and the Holy Spirit].
- Restoration of the Ministry of the Holy Spirit.
- Restoration of the Bible to individual believers.
- Restoration of the baptism and communion to its biblical meaning and application.
- Restoration of the truths of salvation doctrines: sin, the atonement, justification, sanctification and glorification.
- Restoration of the priesthood of all believers.
- Restoration and establishment of the sacred hymns of the church.
- Restoration of foreign missions [worldwide].
- Restoration of the ministry of reconciliation [all believers].

I have but touched the surface of those present truths restored to the Christian church. It is my prayer that each church and believer will assess their current standing. As we serve this present age, are we effective in receiving restored truth from the Holy Spirit and living out our Christian faith while passing the faith and truths of God's Word on to the next generation? Our answer to this question will depend on our worldview, rather biblical or secular. I ask again, what is a worldview?

A worldview is the framework from which we view reality and make sense of life and the world. It is any ideology, philosophy, theology, movement or religion that provides an overarching approach to understanding God, the world and man's relation to God and the world; and says, David Nobel, author of *"Understanding the Times."*[29]

The Role of the Church

It is true that each individual believer is ultimately responsible for ensuring that his or her worldview is in agreement with biblical truth. However, if a church is serious about involvement in the spiritual growth of its people; there are a number of things the church can pursue to insure that the process is available to:

- Assist and motivate each member in developing a viable biblical worldview.
- Provide biblically based teaching that challenges and informs all of the members.
- Accumulate a list of preferable Scriptures and other resources along with an agenda for the members' personal spiritual growth.
- Provide small group, mentorship and one-on-one ministries.
- Develop a means of holding individuals accountable.
- Once young adult believers have developed enough to do so, they should take responsibility to reach and teach other young people. This will provide an opportunity to answer their honest questions and hone your own wisdom.

This list is in no way conclusive; but the essence of all these endeavors is to evaluate your spiritual and biblical growth. The goal is developing a biblical worldview based on the infallible Word of God. When you believe the Bible is entirely true, then you allow it to be the *foundation* of everything you say and do.

Now that we have developed a biblical worldview; it is important to realize that there is also a non-biblical secular worldview. We are constantly bombarded with this worldview from internet, television, movies, music, newspapers, magazines, books and academia.

Citizenship

Some studies show that only half of the Christians are registered to vote and only half of those that are registered actually do vote. God appoints government leaders and it is our duty to elect leaders whom we believe have integrity and represent the issues we feel are most important. According to Romans 13:1-3, it is our duty as citizens to study the issues and the candidates and vote.

> *"Let every soul be subject to the authorities. For there is no authority except from God, and the authorities that exist are appointed by God. Therefore whoever resists the authority resists the ordinance of God, and those who resist will bring judgment on themselves. Rulers are not a terror to good works, but to evil. Do you want to be unafraid of the authority? Do what is good, and you will have praise from the same."*

Government, media, nor the academia elite can change the culture. God's people have to change our culture. Peaceful, law-abiding citizens need not fear the authorities. Few governments will harm those who obey their laws. In fact governments usually commend such people. We have to change culture since it precedes and shapes politics.

Results of a non-biblical Worldview

> *"Trust in the Lord with all your heart and lean not to your own understanding....."* (Proverbs 3:5-6).

Earlier I pointed out the results of a biblical worldview; which can be summarized, "Trust in the Lord!" Not to trust in the Lord means that we "lean on our own understanding." The results of this non-biblical worldview is seen in society through the tremendous amount of suffering, broken families, divorces, illegitimacy in newborns, cohabitation, wasted lives, ineffective Christians and churches. This is exactly opposite to those who belong to the Lord and live a biblical worldview – where He promises, "If you acknowledge Him, He will direct your paths."

STUDY SUMMARY: CHAPTER 18

1. In the last days, we will experience a time of refreshing
   _____ as a result of genuine repentance.
2. A time of _____ precedes the return of the
   Lord Jesus Christ.
3. Restoration is the process of _____ a condition
   through a process of Change.
4. List four faults that infiltrated the church during the first five
   hundred years:
   a.
   b.
   c.
   d.

5. The _____ of the _____
   _____ took place on the
   _____ of _____.
6. List the five ministerial gifts that Christ gave to the church
   below:
   a.
   b.
   c.
   d.
   e.

7. The church eliminated the ministries of the _____,
   then the _____, the _____ and
   the _____.
8. The _____ of man began to have more authority than
   the Word of God.
9. The Protestant Reformation of the sixteenth century ignited a
   _____ _____ that shook the world.
10. The 1100 years between the first five hundred years of the church
    and the Reformation are called the _____ ages.
11. The Protestant Churches came into existence because a Catholic
    priest named _____ _____.

12. _____ by grace through _____ was the major truth restored in the Restoration.

13. Define a "biblical worldview" in the space below:

14. Some studies show that only half of the Christians are registered to vote and only _____ of those that are _____ actually to vote.

15. According to Romans _____ it is a citizen's duty to vote.

CHAPTER 19

FAITH FOR THE FINAL HOUR

"....... When the Son of Man cometh, shall He find
faith on the earth?" (Luke 18:8). KJV

The term "faith" is used very loosely today in every quarter of society and the church. Many equate faith to receiving from a bountiful God in material things especially financial. Others equate it to mean a better quality of life, without sickness or disease. In other words, it's all about me and mine. However, the reference to Jesus' question in this passage is not to personal faith, but to the whole body of revealed truth (see Romans 1:5; 1Cor. 16:13; 2 Cor. 13:5; Col. 1:23; 2:7; Titus 1:13). When Christ returns will His followers still *be* looking for Him? Will we have faith for the final hour?

These two questions seem to point at least to fear since the Second Coming is long delayed, that there would be no clear witness or true faith. All would have died out in the hearts of even the true believers. This is the same outlook in the parable of the ten virgins, when Jesus said, *"they all slumbered and slept,"* both the wise virgins and the foolish (see Matthew 25:5).

The Greek word rendered "faith" in the King James Version is actually the word "faithfulness." All believers want to hear the Lord say, "Well done good and faithful servant: thou hast been faithful over a few things, I will make thee ruler over many things: enter thou into the joy of the Lord" (see Matthew 25:21also Galatians 5:22).

Faithfulness

Most men will proclaim every one his own goodness: but a faithful man who can find? (Proverbs 20:6). KJV

It is very difficult to find a truly faithful person today. Yet this is the very characteristic of Christ that causes the Christian to stand out from the crowd and receive God's focused attention. Therefore, we Christians should desire to develop this segment of the fruit of the Spirit because God is seeking this character quality in His children, who will have faith for the final hour.

The parable of the talents

It was unfaithfulness that caused God to drive Adam and Eve out of the garden of Eden over which he was given dominion (see Genesis 3:23, 24). God made man not only for fellowship, but He also gave him stewardship. Just as it was true of Adam and Eve in the beginning, so it is today, God is still seeking faithful people to whom He can entrust His possessions.

God will bless His people individually with as much as He can responsibly trust them to care for. The Scripture says, "A faithful man [woman] shall abound with blessings........." (Proverbs 28:20).

Who then is a faithful and wise servant, whom his lord hath made ruler over his household, to give them meat in due season?

Blessed is that servant, whom his lord when he cometh shall find so doing.

Verily I say unto you, that he shall make him ruler over all his goods (Matthew 24:45-47). KJV

God cannot trust the gifts of the Spirit, the fruit of the Spirit, the wisdom, the knowledge, and the revelation truths continued in God's Word to many people because they are not found faithful.

The parable of the talents in Matthew 25:14-30 compares the kingdom of heaven with a man who entrusted his servants with his goods before traveling to a far country. To one he gave five talents, to another two talents, and to the third he gave one talent.

When he returned, the master called for an accounting from his servants. He commended the good and faithful servants who had invested what had been entrusted to them and presented them an increase:

- The servant entrusted with five talents presented his lord with ten talents, and heard him say, *"Well done, thou good and faithful servant"* (v. 21).
- The servant entrusted with two talents presented his lord with four talents and also heard the words, *"Well done, good and faithful servant"* (v. 23).
- The servant with the one talent admitted that he had not been faithful with his lord's goods in that through fear he took the one talent entrusted to him and hid it in the ground. Every Christian who is serving the Lord Jesus should be aware of the *spiritual warning* in the response of the lord to the unfaithful servant:

> *"Take therefore the talent from him, and give it*
> *Unto him which hath ten talents.*
> *For unto everyone that hath shall be given, indicates*
> *And he shall have abundance:*
> *But from him that hath not*
> *That which he hath"*

Matthew (25:28, 29). KJV

Notice, the spiritual principle involved here and apply it to your life:

- God will take His goods from the unfaithful servant and give them to the faithful. In verse 29, everyone who has been faithful will receive *more*, but he who has been unfaithful will *lose* even what he does have.

Verse 28 indicates that his goods will be taken from him or [her] by the Lord and bestowed upon someone who will use them wisely for the sake of the kingdom of God.

Therefore, if we Christians today are not faithful with what God has entrusted to us, we should expect Him to take it from us and give it to those who are faithful. Spiritual principles do not change!

An Old Testament example of this forfeiture of a spiritual blessing can be found in the case of Saul:

> *"But the Spirit of the Lord departed from Saul, and an evil spirit from the Lord troubled him"* (1 Samuel 16:14). KJV

Saul had been the Lord's chosen to serve as king of Israel. However, when he proved himself *unfaithful* to that calling, the Lord removed His anointing from him and placed it upon David, the young shepherd boy He knew would be *faithful*.

The Lord Jesus referred to this principle when He told the people of His day:

> *"Therefore say I unto you, the kingdom of God shall be taken from you, and given to a nation bringing forth the fruits thereof"* (Matthew 21:43). KJV

The nation of Israel was not faithful with the revelation of the promised Messiah, so the Lord took the revelation from them and gave it to the Gentiles, a people who would accept it and be faithful to it.

Two classes of unfaithful in the body of Christ

One class of the unfaithful is the believer who once made a commitment to the Lord and was living for Him but who has since backslidden, thus losing the anointing that was upon him or her. If this person will repent and come back to the Lord, the Lord's anointing will return upon them, for God's gifts and callings are without repentance [irrevocable] (see Romans 11:29).

The next class of the unfaithful is those believers who are not faithful with their God-given gifts and callings – so needed in kingdom life and ministry today, but they stand in danger of losing them. There are those in the Body of Christ who:

- Have the gift of intercession, but won't use it.
- Have the gift of prophecy or proclamation, but won't stir up the gift that is within them.
- Have the gift of teaching, but will not take the time to study, get into that Word and dig out the treasures of wisdom and knowledge which are contained therein.
- Have the gift of the word of knowledge, but will not bring it forth.
- Have a gift or gifts but, put them secondary in importance to their worldly pursuits. [For example I knew a professional educator who desired to pursue a calling to preach the gospel, but wanted to wait a few years until retirement]. It never came to past.
- Have the gift of helps, but won't get involved.

It is definitely a spiritual principle that God will take the gifts from those who are *unfaithful* and will give them to those who are *faithful*. Such unfaithful servants need to be very careful or they may find themselves in the same predicament as Esau: *For ye know how that afterward, when he would have inherited the blessing, he was rejected: for he found no place of repentance, though he sought it carefully with tears* (Hebrews 12:17). KJV

Pleasing to God

According to the New Testament, faith pleases God: *But without faith it is impossible to please Him: for he that cometh to God must believe that He is and that He is a rewarder of them that diligently seek Him* (Hebrews 11:6). KJV

In John 8:29 Jesus said that He always did those things that pleased His Father. To say it another way, Jesus was always faithful.

Therefore, if we are going to have faith for the final hour – being faithful to God should be the most important goal in the Christian's life. Yet much of the busy work we are doing is really our own thing done in His name. It has never dawned on many Christians individually and corporately that God is more interested in faithfulness than He is in accomplishment. His concern is not how much the child of God achieves in life as much as it is whether or not he or she is doing what He has told them to do.

I read a story concerning a Christian man who was appointed president of a very prestigious university a few days before he was to take his post his wife suffered a severe stroke which would require much care for she would not be able to walk again and she had lost part of her brain function. After much prayer, he did not take the position, why? He said the Lord told him to go home and care for his wife. People would have understood if he had hired a couple of nurses to take around the clock care of his wife especially on the salary he was to receive. In spite of all the other scenarios, he chose to be faithful and please God by obeying and doing what He told him to do.

Contend for the Faith

In Jude 3, the writer admonishes that Christians should, "......... contend for *the faith* which was once delivered unto the saints. For there are certain men crept in unawares, who were before of old ordained to this condemnation, ungodly men, turning the grace of God into lasciviousness, and denying the only Lord God, and our Lord Jesus Christ."

The Church of Jesus Christ must come to understand that the word *faith* means *faithfulness* and that the reason we contend for and stand in faith is that by doing so we are being faithful to God, and therefore pleasing Him. The Church must understand that faith is the only way anyone can ever truly please God the Father. This is the faith for the final hour!

Cultivating the Faith

All believers have the seed of faithfulness within their born-again spirits. But they must learn to develop it both as individuals and as the body of Christ as a whole. Jesus said, *"He that is faithful in that which is least is faithful also in much: and he who is unjust in the least is unjust also in much"* (Luke 16:10).

The word *least* is not used here in the sense of lesser than, but compared with everything else, in the sense of the least of the amount of affairs.[30] When a Christian demonstrates that he or she is faithful with the least of their possessions, God can bestow more important possessions upon them.

Developing a trust between ourselves and our God so that we know that the Lord Himself actually trusts us and has *faith* in us is assurance that the Son of man will find faith on the earth when He comes.

STUDY SUMMARY: CHAPTER 19

1. The Greek word rendered "faith" is actually the word _____.
2. It us very difficult to find a _____ person today.
3. Christ is seeking those who desire this segment of the _____ of _____ _____.
4. _____ caused God to drive Adam and Eve out of the Garden of Eden.
5. God cannot trust the following gifts to many because they are not found faithful listed below:
    a.
    b.
    c.
    d.
    e.

6. The parable of the talents compares the kingdom of God with a man who _____ his _____ with his _____.
7. He gave one _____ talents, another _____ and a third one with _____ talents.
8. Briefly explain in the space below, the principle of unfaithfulness:
9. Explain below God's action taken for Saul's unfaithfulness:
10. Jesus used the principle in Matthew _____ chapter and _____ verse.
11. Spiritual principles do not _____.
12. The Nation of Israel was not _____ with the _____ of the _____ _____.
13. Briefly explain how God handles the backslider in the space below:
14. Briefly explain how God handles those who are unfaithful with their gifts:
15. Explain briefly the usage of the word "least" in Luke 16:10:

INTRODUCTION

1   Webster's New Explorer Dictionary and Thesaurus (Merriam-Webster, Inc. 1999) page 479.

Chapter 1

2   Lawerance O. Richards, *A Theology of Church Leadership* (The Zondovan Corporation 1980) 66
3   Derek Prince, *Foundational Truth for Christian Living* (Charisma House 2006) 292-293
4   Jay R. Leach, *How Should We Then Live* (iUniverse Publishers 2010) 93
5   Ibid.
6   Ray C. Stedman, *Body Life* (Discovery House Books 1995 revised edition by Elaine Stedman) 15
7   W. E. Vines, *New Testament Greek Grammar and Dictionary* (Thomas Nelson 2012) 442
8   Ibid.

Chapter 6

9   Andrew Murray, *Abide in Christ* (Barbour and Company Publishers 1992) 100
10 Ibid.

Chapter 7

11 Lawrence O. Richards – page 17
12 Ibid.
13 Henry T. Blackaby and Claude V. King, *Experiencing God* (Broadman and Holman Publishers 1994) page 223.

Chapter 8

14 The word "power" carries the connotation of meaning to "blow up" (as happens with dynamite), but it also refers to "dynamo" which produces power as needed. It produces a gradual buildup of power. The Greek term is *dunamus,* carrying the definition of our word "dynamo."
15 Adapted from the introductory notes on the Book of Ephesians in the *New King James Version Study Bible* (Thomas Nelson Publishers 2007) 1858
16 Jay R. Leach, (Taken from my Lecture notes "Spiritual Gifts and Ministry," a course I've taught for the past sixteen years at the Bread of Life Bible Institute.

Chapter 9

17 Adapted from the Teacher's Outline & Study Bible by Alpha-Omega Ministries (1996) 109

Chapter 10

18 Henry T. Blackaby & Claude V. King page 39
19 Lawrence O. Richards – adapted from pages 89-93
20 Jay R. Leach, *Grace that Saves* (Trafford Publishing 2014) 108-112 as accessed from Secular Humanism.org/index.php 10/19/13

Chapter 14

21 Webster's New Explorer Dictionary and Thesaurus (Merriam-Webster Inc. 1999) 403
22 George Barna, *Futurecast* (Tyndale House Publishers, Inc. 2011) 227
23 Accessed: http://.barna.org/barna update/millenials/682-5ways-to-connect-with-millennials 9/12/14

Chapter 15

24   Dwight Perry, *Building Unity in the Church of the New Millennium.* An edited interview with Evelyn Christenson, *Is there a Place for Elderly Saints in the body of Christ)*Moody Press, 2002) 253

Chapter 17

25   John Dewey, *A Common Faith (The Terry Lecture Series)* (New Haven: Yale University Press, 1934) cover.

26   Charles Francis Potter, *(Humanism: A New Religion* (New York: Simon and Schuster, 1930), 128.

Chapter 18

27   Hector Torres, *The Restoration of the Apostle* (Thomas Nelsons Publishers, Inc. 2001) 8

28   Dr. Bill Hamon, *The Day of the Saints* (Destiny Image 2002) adapted from pages 156-159

29   Accessed   http://www.focusonthefamily.com/faith/christian-worldview/whats-a-christian-worldview.... 11/11/14.

Chapter 19

30   W.E. Vine's Greek Grammar and Dictionary, page 430